LET'S ROLL!

Ordinary People,
Extraordinary Courage

LISA BEAMER
with Ken Abraham

TYNDALE HOUSE PUBLISHERS, INC., WHEATON, ILLINOIS

Visit Tyndale's exciting Web site at www.tyndale.com

For appearances and other inquiries for Lisa Beamer, contact www.lbeamer.com or call 1-800-927-0517.

Editor, Ramona Cramer Tucker

Acquisitions Director, Tammy Faxel

Designer, Jenny Swanson

Published in association with the literary agency of Alive Communications, Inc., 7680 Goddard Street, Suite 200, Colorado Springs, CO 80920.

Printed in the United States of America

09 08 07 06 05 04 03 02
8   7   6   5   4   3   2   1

To Todd,
my husband, my everyday hero.
Thank you for loving God, loving us, and always playing hard.
Thank you for teaching me patience and mercy.
I love you and promise to finish our journey well.
See you later. . . .

CONTENTS

CHAPTER 1 . . . . *A Day We'll Never Forget* 1

CHAPTER 2 . . . . *Salt-of-the-Earth Folks* 13

CHAPTER 3 . . . . *The "Go-To" Guy* 21

CHAPTER 4 . . . . *Our Paths Cross . . .* 33

CHAPTER 5 . . . . *A Norman Rockwell World* 41

CHAPTER 6 . . . . *Wrestling with the "Whys"* 59

CHAPTER 7 . . . . *Stepping Out on Faith* 75

CHAPTER 8 . . . . *Surprised by Love* 85

CHAPTER 9 . . . . *Forward Thinking* 97

CHAPTER 10 . . . . *Adding to Our Team* 111

CHAPTER 11 . . . . *Trouble at the Top* 123

CHAPTER 12 . . . . *Living the Dream* 139

CHAPTER 13 . . . . *Roman Holiday* 147

CHAPTER 14 . . . *A Whirlwind Arrival—and Departure* 157

CHAPTER 15 . . . . *Inside the Nightmare* 163

CHAPTER 16 . . . . *How to Tell the Children?* 175

CHAPTER 17 . . . . *A Phone Call from Heaven* 181

CHAPTER 18 . . . . *Reliving the Takeover* 189

CHAPTER 19 . . . . *Plots aboard Flight 93* 199

CHAPTER 20. . . . . *A Team United . . . in Life and Death*   209

CHAPTER 21 . . . *Saying Good-Bye to Todd . . . for Now*   219

CHAPTER 22 . . . . *The Shanksville Crash Site*   227

CHAPTER 23 . . . . *It's Just Me!*   237

CHAPTER 24 . *Poignant Moments . . . and Key Decisions*   255

CHAPTER 25 . *The "Completed" Flight to San Francisco*   263

CHAPTER 26. . . . . *The Reason for My Hope*   273

CHAPTER 27 . . . . *Life Goes On . . . or Does It?*   279

CHAPTER 28 . . . . *Welcoming Morgan*   287

CHAPTER 29 . . . . *The Bigger Picture*   295

CHAPTER 30 . . . . *It Is Well with My Soul*   307

All the Heroes of United Flight 93   313

The Todd M. Beamer Foundation   316

About the Authors   319

A DAY WE'LL
NEVER FORGET

THE RINGING OF AN ALARM CLOCK dragged me
reluctantly from a deep sleep at 5:45 A.M. on Tuesday,
September 11. My husband, Todd, rolled over and silenced
the annoying noise. I roused slightly, peeking out from
under the covers only long enough to notice it was still dark
outside. Although I wasn't ready to get up yet, I knew the
bright morning sunshine would soon be streaming through
the bay window in our bedroom. Pulling the covers up over
my head, I attempted to go back to sleep.

We had just returned from Rome, Italy, late afternoon the
previous day, so between the jet lag and the strain of being
five months pregnant, a few extra minutes of sleep seemed
like a good idea. I anticipated a full day ahead of me. Besides
keeping up with our two energetic boys—David, our three-
and-a-half-year-old, and Drew, who was 19 months—I had
numerous tasks to accomplish. The laundry had stacked up.
I needed to stop by the bank and then go to the grocery store
to replenish the refrigerator we had cleaned out before going

1

away. After that I had several more errands to run. David would be starting preschool tomorrow, so I wanted to talk with him about the transition in our lives that "school" would bring. My to-do list grew longer even in my sleep as I remembered all the things I had to take care of after being away from home for a week. Vacation was over; life was back to normal. I sighed inwardly.

Todd eased out of bed, trying his best not to disturb me as he headed toward the shower. As one of the top young sales representatives of the software giant Oracle Corporation, Todd traveled a lot for business as well as for pleasure. His job often required whirlwind trips, so to him, this early-morning flight was just another day at the office—a one-day jaunt to San Francisco to meet with some high-profile clients. He'd catch the red-eye flight home that same night.

"I can do it. It's no big deal," he'd said when he informed me of his plans to travel so soon after our return from Europe. "I'll be back before you know it."

Somewhere between being asleep and awake that Tuesday morning, I heard the shower running. A short time later I vaguely sensed Todd leaning over me and kissing me good-bye, as he always did before leaving for the day. Sometimes I'd have the covers pulled up so high he'd have to kiss the top of my head. That's what he must have done that morning, because we didn't communicate verbally—or if we did, I don't remember it.

I heard Todd's footsteps going down the hardwood back steps and smiled to myself as I imagined him trying to walk quietly. When we'd built our new home little more than a year earlier, I hadn't wanted to carpet the steps because I didn't want to vacuum them! But the price I paid for that decision was hearing the clomping of footsteps any time Todd left for one of his predawn trips.

I snuggled a little farther down, burying myself beneath the blankets. The sun would be up soon, and the boys would rise shortly after that. *Better get some last-minute sleep while I can.*

By 6:45 the sun was indeed shining brightly through our bedroom window, so I hopped out of bed. It was a gorgeous blue-sky morning—not a cloud to be seen and unseasonably warm for September in New Jersey. *What a beautiful day!* I thought. *Maybe the boys and I will have some time to play outside later.*

A habitual list maker, I started going over my grocery list, adding needed items and trying to get organized before the boys got up. I had just begun folding some laundry when I heard the patter of a little boy's bare feet coming down the front staircase.

"Good morning, David!" I hugged him in his pajamas. Drew waddled behind David in the telltale manner every mother of toddlers knows all too well. "Come on, Drew. Let's get that diaper changed before we have breakfast."

It was a full-tilt morning, per usual life for a family with young children.

The boys sat up at our breakfast bar, and I got them some Froot Loops and Cheerios to eat. Later, after they'd eaten and dressed, they watched *Sesame Street* while I went upstairs for a quick shower.

A few minutes after nine o'clock, as I was getting ready to go to the grocery store, the phone rang. I ignored it since

I was about to walk out the door. But our answering machine picked up the call, and I heard the familiar voice of my friend Elaine Mumau. She sounded stressed.

"Hi, Lisa. I know Todd is traveling today . . . and I was just calling to check on him. . . . Do you have your television turned on? . . . Have you seen what's happening?"

I grabbed the phone. "Elaine, what are you talking about?"

"Isn't Todd flying today?"

"Yes, he is. Why?"

"Do you know his flight number?"

"No, I don't. Why, Elaine? What's going on?"

"Turn the TV on," Elaine instructed. "There's been a plane crash at the World Trade Center."

I turned on the television and saw the Twin Towers enveloped in a huge plume of smoke. A second plane had just smashed into one of the towers, tearing a gaping hole in the building and setting it ablaze. Commentators described the scene in shocked, pensive tones. I stood in front of our television, mesmerized by the horrific sight. Before long the newscasters reported that two planes—an American Airlines flight and a United Airlines flight—were missing and might have been the ones that hit the towers. The broadcasters speculated about possible terrorist involvement in the crashes.

I had no idea what flight Todd was on; I didn't even know what airline he was flying that morning. He traveled so much that I'd long ago given up pressing him for travel itineraries. Most Oracle sales reps booked their travel on-line, so I didn't even have a travel agent to call for information. But I knew Todd was going to San Francisco. And since he often flew Continental Airlines on that route, I breathed a slight sigh of relief.

Nevertheless, as I stared in disbelief at the events unfolding live on television, my heart began pounding faster. *Oh, those poor people!* I thought. *How can this be happening?!*

Although unsure of Todd's whereabouts, I really wasn't too worried about his safety. My husband was a seasoned traveler, and over the years he'd learned how to deal with almost any situation frequent air travelers encounter—delayed flights, missed flights, canceled flights, mechanical problems, airline strikes—you name it, he'd had to work around it. By now we'd been married for more than seven years. Earlier in our marriage I'd sometimes been overly agitated when Todd was late coming home, or when I learned of an airline incident or a bad accident on the highway in an area where Todd was traveling. My mind had immediately conjured up all sorts of awful images. But Todd had always come out fine, and after a while I stopped worrying about him so much. Neither of us had any fear of flying; in fact, we often joked that the most dangerous part of our travel was the trek on the New Jersey Turnpike between our home in Cranbury, near Princeton, and the Newark airport.

Besides, Todd was a gadget nut who carried two cellular phones with him constantly—one in the car and one on his person. I nearly had to wrestle those phones out of his hands every time we went on vacation. If Todd was delayed or in any trouble, he'd call.

Still, I was uneasy. I dialed the phone number for Continental Airlines, and, amazingly, got through to a customer service representative right away. I was among the lucky ones. Many calls were being disconnected that day—partially due to the overloaded systems with so many people making calls, but also because so much of the communications system for the tristate area had been located atop the World Trade Center towers. Cellular calls fared little better than landlines for the same reasons.

The Continental representative refused to tell me whether Todd was aboard one of their planes, but he did say that their 7:00 A.M. flight had departed Newark with no problems. The second flight hadn't yet left the terminal because the Federal Aviation Administration had grounded all flights until further notice.

I knew that if Todd's flight hadn't taken off, he would have called me, so I assumed he was safely aboard the earlier flight. *Okay, there's no need to worry,* I assured myself as I hung up the phone. *Todd's probably halfway across the country by now.*

A few minutes later it occurred to me that Todd hadn't left the house until around 6:15. Even on a good traffic day, Newark International Airport is a 30-minute drive from our home—not counting delays due to the perpetual construction at the aging airport. That certainly didn't allow Todd much time if he had booked the early Continental flight. My stomach churned as I recalled that Todd sometimes flew United Airlines to San Francisco. *I'd better call them, just to check,* I assured myself.

Completing a phone call was becoming ever more difficult. I paced back and forth while waiting through busy signals and negotiating the phone-tree maze, hoping to reach a human being. I was disappointed. United Airlines representatives were all "helping other customers." I was soon to find out why.

Increasingly frustrated in my attempts to get any information about my husband, I was growing more anxious by the minute. Finally I called Elaine back.

Her husband, Brian, was working at home and answered the phone. I told him of my failed efforts and asked, "Can you try to find out what flight Todd is on? I just can't do it right now."

Brian must have sensed my uneasiness. "Sure, Lisa. Let me see what I can find out. I'll get right on it."

"Thanks, Brian."

"Lisa? Elaine is going to come over."

I hung up the phone, turned away from the television set, and walked back to the laundry room, where despite my best efforts to maintain composure, I burst into tears. When David came in and saw me crying, he asked, "What's wrong, Mommy?"

"It's okay," I answered, trying to hold back the tears. "I just don't know where Daddy is right now. But don't worry. We'll find him. I'm sure he's fine; I just don't know what's going on."

David returned to his toys, and I picked up the phone again. I dialed Todd's business cell-phone number and listened to his voice as his prerecorded message played through. "You've reached Todd Beamer with the Oracle Corporation. Please leave a message."

I left a message. "Todd, I know you're fine. But when you land, please call me right away. I don't know where you are and I need to hear from you."

■　■　■　■

A few minutes later my phone rang. Hoping it was Todd on the line, I hurried out to the kitchen to answer it. "Hello!"

There was no answer. The line had gone dead. I glanced at the digital clock on our kitchen oven. It was 10:00 A.M.

I took the phone with me back to the laundry room. A few seconds later the phone rang again. I quickly picked up the receiver, but the phone had already stopped ringing. "Hello! Hello?" I nearly screamed into the phone. Disconnected again!

Todd! Where are you?

In my wildest imagination—or my worst nightmares—I couldn't possibly have dreamed what Todd was actually experiencing at that precise moment.

■　■　■　■

Soon afterward, Elaine and her three children arrived. She and I went into our family room and sat down on the couch in front of the television while the kids headed for the playroom. Just then the network switched from New York to Washington, D.C., and scenes from the Pentagon came up on the screen. Another airliner had crashed into the side of our nation's military headquarters around 9:43 A.M., and the awful curl of thick black smoke had already risen high into the otherwise clear skies above the city.

And then the unthinkable happened. While rescue workers feverishly attempted to get people down and out of the World Trade Center, the south tower collapsed. Its steel girders, superheated by the ferocious jet-fuel fire, literally melted and crumbled in a massive, mangled heap. Less than half an hour later the north tower collapsed, releasing a horrendous cloud of smoke, ash, debris, and dust. Surreal scenes of ash-covered people running through the streets filled the television screen.

Now, like most Americans, I was reeling, attempting to comprehend the reality of what I had seen and the enormity of the destruction and loss of life. Questions I feared to ask aloud raced through my mind. *Are there any survivors? Are there more attacks to come? How many more planes are out there with terrorists aboard?* My heart hurt for the unknown number of victims, and my concern for my own husband mounted. I fretted inwardly. *Where's Todd?*

At first Elaine and I sat on the couch with our eyes and ears riveted to the television set. Though shaken by the attacks on our nation and deeply grieved over the loss of life, I remained relatively calm until the networks showed yet another downed airliner. This one had crashed in a field in Pennsylvania. I knew that Todd's flight would have traveled in that general direction. Cold shivers ran through my body, and a sick sensation clutched at my stomach as I gazed in horror at the crash site. Smoke still hovered in the air, and even from a distance I could see the charred ground. It was obvious the plane had been obliterated. No one could survive that sort of impact.

The newscaster's subdued voice reported that the downed flight was a United Airlines flight that had been bound for Chicago.

Chicago? Whew! Again I felt a rush of compassion for those people aboard the plane and their families, but I breathed a little easier for our family. We were off the hook again. Todd had an afternoon meeting in San Francisco; he wouldn't have had time for a layover. So surely he wouldn't have booked anything other than a direct flight.

I got up nervously and stepped behind the couch, still staring at the television, when the newscaster's voice intoned, "We have an update on the airliner that has crashed in Pennsylvania. It was not en route to Chicago as previously reported; it was actually a United flight out of Newark that was going to San Francisco."

"No!" I screamed helplessly at the television.

Without a shred of hard evidence, I knew intuitively that Todd was on that flight. Suddenly I felt as though my body weighed a million pounds; it seemed my heart might explode. I fell to my hands and knees and gasped again, "No!"

In an instant Elaine joined me on the floor, wrapping her arms around me. "It's probably not his flight, Lisa. He's probably fine. We don't know what's what. Don't worry. Todd's okay."

"No, Elaine . . . that's his plane," I managed to say through my tears.

"We don't know that. . . ."

I'd seen enough. In my heart I knew. I couldn't watch any longer. "I'm going to go upstairs now. . . . Please watch the boys for a while." Elaine assured me that she would. I made my way to my bedroom and sat down on the edge of the bed, staring out the window in a near-catatonic state. I didn't move; I didn't speak. It was as though time had come to an abrupt halt, and I no longer existed. In a desperate, futile attempt to make sense of it all, my heart and mind had temporarily shut down. I was numb. I could see and hear, yet I simply continued to stare straight ahead.

Surely this can't be happening, I thought. *It must just be a bad dream. Todd can't be gone! Maybe there's some mistake.*

But the grim reality pinched at any idealism or hope of a miracle that I might have momentarily embraced. *What now? What are we going to do?* I thought of our boys, David and Drew, who loved their daddy so dearly and were now getting to the ages where they could romp and play with him as a trio of Beamer boys. Todd loved playing with our kids. I touched my bulging belly and thought of the new life I carried inside—Todd's and my third child, due in mid-January. *Oh, God, how am I going to do this?* I agonized inwardly. Our life was so good; we had so many plans. I *needed* Todd. He always made everything okay.

In that dark moment, my soul cried out to God—and he began to give me a sense of peace and a confidence that the children and I were going to be okay. But even that comfort didn't take away the wrenching pain or the awful sense of loss I felt. Nor did it answer the question that continually tugged at my heart: *How can I live without Todd?*

In my braver moments, I dared to ponder what Todd might have experienced aboard that plane before it had gone down. I wondered if he had been injured . . . or possibly even killed by the terrorists. I felt strongly that Todd's final thoughts and expressions would have been of his faith in God and his love for his family. And I knew in my heart, if there were any way possible, that he wouldn't have gone down without a fight.

Even before we met as college students, Todd had been the "go-to" guy, the person everyone expected to make things happen. And usually he did! Todd Beamer always came through in the clutch. That's just the sort of guy he was. . . .

2

SALT-OF-THE-EARTH FOLKS

MAKING THINGS HAPPEN came naturally to Todd. He knew that in order to enjoy success in any area—athletics, business, or relationships—he had to work hard, create smart strategies, and be a team player. No doubt many of these disciplines were acquired by observing his dad, David Beamer, who had learned these same lessons long before Todd was born.

Of German-English stock, David grew up on a dairy farm outside Homeworth, Ohio, a small town of about 500 people. David's parents, John and Wanda Beamer, were godly, "salt-of-the-earth" folks—hard workers who thought nothing of getting up long before daybreak and working long past sundown. David and his younger sister, Bonnie, assumed that same work ethic, getting up before school to milk the cows and do other chores.

While in high school, David met Peggy Jackson, an attractive young woman of Pennsylvania Dutch descent. She had grown up in Sebring, Ohio, a small pottery town between Canton and Youngstown, close to the Ohio Turn-pike. There her dad owned and operated an electrical repair shop, where he worked on generators, starters, the electrical systems of cars, and the tractor-trailer trucks that encountered engine problems while traveling the turnpike. His name was George Edward Jackson, but everyone—including his wife, Evelyn—called him "Judd." Nobody knew just why the name stuck, nor could anyone remember ever calling Peggy's dad by any name other than Judd Jackson.

The youngest of three children, including her brother, Ed, and sister, Dorothy Jean (Fawley), Peggy was soft-spoken. Yet her infectious smile and warm, gracious personality drew others to her.

Peggy and David met during their freshman year. Peggy was the head majorette in the band, and David was the drummer. "She blew the whistle and told me what to do," David recalls. A fellow band member played match-maker, suggesting, "You two need to be a couple."

David and Peggy concurred. They dated throughout high school and then married when David was only midway through his college program in electrical engineering at Ohio State University. He was 21, and Peggy, a year younger. "We struck a deal," David remembers. "She'd work to help us make ends meet while I went to school, and when I graduated, she could stay home and I'd go get a real job!" The deal worked. David went on to earn his master's in business, and eventually Peggy became a stay-at-home mom.

Three years after they married, the couple moved to Florida, where David's first job out of college was with

NASA, the U.S. space program, at Cape Canaveral. "I was part of the program to make sure that America didn't fall too far behind the Soviet Union in the space race," says David, only half-joking.

The couple's first child, Melissa, was born in 1966 at Cape Canaveral Hospital. When Peggy became pregnant again early in 1968, David felt he could better provide for his family by moving to Flint, Michigan, where he went to work for IBM. The family settled in the small town of Flushing, just northwest of Flint. That's where Todd Morgan Beamer was born on November 24, 1968. Todd was simply a name David and Peggy liked, and Morgan was Peggy's grandfather's name. Michele, the youngest Beamer, came along in 1974.

The family lived in the Flint area for six years and were actively involved at Calvary Baptist Church. These were busy years, spent managing a home, young children, and David's growing career. The church provided important friendships as well as solid teaching from the Bible on values and priorities. But for the Beamers, God wasn't just for Sundays. David and Peggy brought God into their home, encouraging the children not only to *read* the Bible but also to *apply* what they learned to daily life. And David and Peggy modeled to the children that they could talk to God in prayer *anytime.*

As a child, Todd loved to pray before bedtime—not because he was super-spiritual, but because he discovered early on that the longer he prayed, the longer David and Peggy allowed him to stay awake! Kneeling down beside his bed, Todd would look around his room and then cast his gaze beyond, to the rooms outside his. He'd thank God for everything in each room that he could see—the curtains, the beds, the walls, the bathtub, the carpet, and on and on. "After a while, I opened my eyes and realized he was taking inventory of the entire house!" recalls Peggy.

Even when young, Todd believed in the power of prayer to impact events and circumstances. Once he and his five-year-old friend Keith Simpson found a toad and were playing with it. Somehow the toad escaped their grasp, and the boys searched everywhere for their brackish, green friend, to no avail. At suppertime they agreed to pray that God would help them find the toad. Keith went into his room to pray and Todd headed home. Todd had no sooner stepped in the door when Keith's mom phoned. She reported that after Keith prayed, he'd walked out the back door and found the toad. To Todd, it was a miracle that ranked right up there alongside the healing of a blind man or the raising of Lazarus from the dead!

Each morning before school, while the children were eating breakfast, Peggy read them a chapter from the book of Proverbs. From this book the children learned biblical principles of ethics and morality, and plenty of practical advice.

Peggy and David raised Todd and the girls with a strong biblical value system and work ethic. "Hard work pays off. Do your best and you'll succeed; hold true to your faith and you'll be okay," they taught their children. Along with that, Todd's parents modeled respect for themselves and others, taught the importance of boundaries and taking responsibility, and exhibited compassionate hearts. They made it clear that discipline mattered in the Beamer family, too.

Since David traveled a great deal for his job, Peggy often found herself in the role of disciplinarian. The Beamer kids were taught from an early age that "no means no!" Peggy was not one to say, "Wait till your dad gets home." Whenever the kids needed discipline and correction, she provided it.

Once, for example, when Todd was three or four years old, he talked back to his mom. Peggy washed his mouth out with soap. Apparently, however, modern-day soap didn't taste quite as repugnant as the kind Peggy's mom had used with her. Todd looked up at her after she'd rinsed out his mouth and said, "Mmm-mmm, tastes like soap!"

Even as a youngster, Todd had some unusual tastes when it came to food. Peggy had a tradition of making whatever meal the kids wanted on their birthday. He could have asked for prime rib, lobster, or other delicacies. But Todd always asked for sauerkraut and hot dogs. "Anything but lima beans!" he said.

Todd and Melissa both loved chocolate, and Grandma Beamer made the best chocolate brownies this side of Betty Crocker. She also made a mean chocolate cake with brown-sugar frosting that tasted just like smooth fudge. One day when Todd was about five years old and Melissa seven, their Aunt Bonnie was visiting, so Grandma Beamer made one of her famous cakes. Grandma Beamer carefully applied the special frosting and then offered Melissa, Bonnie, and Todd the best gift any chocolate lover could ever imagine. "Here are three spoons," she said, nodding toward the leftover frosting in the bowl.

Todd and Melissa immediately started arguing over who

would get to scoop out some delicious chocolate frosting first, so Aunt Bonnie decided to teach them a lesson about sharing. With the skill of a seasoned pro, Aunt Bonnie grabbed her spoon, scraped a pile of leftover frosting onto it, plopped it into her mouth, and ate it in one giant bite.

For a long moment Todd and Melissa stared at her incredulously as if to say, *Aunt Bonnie! How could you do such a thing?*

Then, suddenly, Todd began to laugh. He laughed and laughed, and before long Melissa was, too. Then Bonnie herself convulsed in laughter. About the time everyone calmed down, Bonnie smacked her lips, and Todd doubled over in renewed gales. His contagious mirth sent everyone reeling again. It was a classic "Todd" moment.

While Todd was competitive with his big sister, Melissa, he was more of an encourager to his little sister, Michele. Michele looked up to Todd from the time she was born, always vying for her brother's attention. One day when she was just a baby, Michele crawled in front of Todd while he was lying on the floor watching television with Melissa. Todd moved Michele out of the way, but a short time later she crawled right back over in front of Todd again, blocking his view of the screen. If Todd moved slightly to the right, Michele moved to the right. If he moved to the left, she moved in front of him again. It was as though even as a baby, Michele was saying, *Hey, big brother! You don't need to look at that TV; look at me!*

Todd did, too. Six years older than Michele, he loved looking out for her and was glad to listen to her questions and offer suggestions. Even after the sister and brother became adults, Michele called Todd often for advice and encouragement. She respected his opinion and his insights more than anyone else's, and he was always willing to offer both.

Meanwhile, Todd's father, David, continued to excel as a sales representative, prompting a promotion and a transfer to Poughkeepsie, New York. Two years later he took a job in Chicago with Amdahl Corporation, another computer technology company, and the family started packing again.

They found a home in Glen Ellyn, a suburb west of Chicago. It was what they were looking for—a town with lots of families . . . and lots of baseball fields. Their new house was close to the First Christian Church and only a mile from Wheaton Christian Grammar School, a private elementary school. Also close by was Wheaton College, a Christian liberal arts school best known for alumni such as Billy Graham, the martyred missionary Jim Elliot, and present-day Speaker of the U.S. House of Representatives, Dennis Hastert. It was the school where Todd would later earn his bachelor's degree.

Wheaton was a great place for Todd Beamer to be, for there he learned many lessons that would impact the rest of his life—and an entire nation.

3

THE "GO-TO" GUY

IN A MEMORY BOOK that Todd created while a student at Wheaton Christian Grammar School, he wrote, "I like gym the best, and I like music the worst." That part of his personality never changed. Todd enjoyed good music, but performing it really wasn't his forte. In his memory book he noted that his favorite song was Elvis Presley's "(You Ain't Nothin' but a) Hound Dog." A music teacher once asked him to direct the choir, waving his arms in front of the entire class. "I could never figure out if the teacher put him in that position to direct or just to keep him from singing!" quipped Peggy, his mom.

During elementary school, Todd took music lessons and learned the rudiments of piano, drums, and trumpet. But it was clear practicing music wasn't his first love. One day Peggy heard Todd pounding out his piano lesson and recognized that the song wasn't sounding quite right. She peeked in the practice room and there was Todd, lying on his back, banging out the tune with his feet on the piano

keys! That was the end of Todd's music lessons. As his little
sister, Michele, developed a love of music performance,
Todd cheered her on, happy that someone else was putting
the piano to good use.

Todd much preferred *his* performance to be on the
athletic field. David and Peggy encouraged Todd to use his
natural ability, to always be coachable, and to practice hard
no matter what sport he was playing. Baseball, basketball,
and soccer were his favorites. Todd joined Little League
at age nine, playing shortstop, center field, and pitcher.
Melissa, his older sister, played basketball and softball and
was almost as much of a sports fan as Todd. When they
couldn't stay up late enough to watch the World Series,
they quizzed Peggy on the game's box scores the following
morning. Todd was an avid fan of the Chicago Bulls, wearing number 23 even before Michael Jordan made it famous.
He also was a fan of the Chicago Bears, but he had a special
place in his heart for the Cubs. It was a rare treat for Todd
and Melissa when the family attended a Chicago Cubs
game at Wrigley Field.

Todd loved to see the Chicago teams win. Making sure
his *own* teams won was important, too, and he took his
performance seriously. Even as a boy of 12, Todd was the
guy people looked to in a clutch. Once in a Little League
game, the manager tapped Todd to come in as a relief pitcher
in the last inning, with two outs and the bases loaded. Todd
bore down hard, hoping to save the game. But he gave up a
base on balls and walked in the winning run.

Todd was devastated. He hung his head and slouched his
shoulders. He felt that he'd let down his team when they

were depending on him. As he walked away from the ball field, his dad caught up with him. "You can't win every game," David consoled him, putting an arm around his son. "You can only do your best. No one wins all the time. We have to move on."

As Todd's demeanor brightened slightly, David continued. "You were in a tough spot out there. But if you're never in a tough situation, it's probably because nobody believes you can handle it. Your coach believed in you. He trusted you to do your best, and you did. That's all anybody can ask." That was exactly what Todd needed to hear. Then he was ready to risk victory or defeat again.

On the Fourth of July, the Beamer family could almost always be found at one of Todd's baseball games. Little League all-star games and other tournaments began over Independence Day, and Todd usually played in multiple games before his team was eliminated from the national competition. Like most Little Leaguers, one of Todd's dreams was to make it to Williamsport, Pennsylvania, to play in the Little League World Series.

Even though he never made it to the World Series, Todd was happy. He'd enjoyed lots of success in his life already. One of his buddies at the Grammar School, Brian Funck, remembers Todd as a good, well-rounded guy. "I secretly wished I could be Todd. He was taller than I was, and everybody liked him, especially the girls. He was really coordinated and seemed to be good at every sport. Everybody picked Todd first for their team."

Todd could handle a basketball well, and the junior high girls were duly impressed. One day he was practicing basketball in the gymnasium with a girl friend, trying to wow her, and broke his ankle. He had to be in a cast and couldn't play ball for six weeks! For a while after that incident he avoided all girls . . . though not for long.

Besides his athletic talents, Todd was known for many other things, including his ability to fall asleep almost anywhere—and sleep soundly. He caught catnaps any time he had the opportunity. During the winter of Todd's seventh-grade year, David and Peggy planned to take their older daughter, Melissa, on a special trip with them. Before leaving, they put Todd and Michele on a plane to Youngstown, Ohio, with a connecting flight to the Akron-Canton airport. There Todd and Michele were to spend a few days with Peggy's parents. The weather was cold and icy when Todd and Michele boarded the flight, but Todd wasn't worried. As soon as he settled into his seat aboard the plane, he nodded off to sleep. The plane pitched and heaved through the bad weather, and Michele held on for dear life, but Todd hardly stirred.

Finally the plane landed at Youngstown and started sliding down the runway . . . and sliding . . . and sliding. In fact, it slid all the way *off* the runway! People aboard the plane yelled hysterically all around Todd and Michele, scaring her to death. But Todd slept through the whole thing! Michele had to poke him with a pencil to wake him up.

■ ■ ■ ■

David and Peggy wanted their children to enjoy fun and games but also to learn the importance of a strong work ethic and how to manage time and money. So they encouraged the children to apply for summer jobs and earn their own spending money.

During the summer following Todd's completion of seventh grade, Todd and Brian Funck worked for Mr. Greiff, the head of maintenance at Wheaton Christian Grammar School. Their responsibilities included stripping and waxing floors, running the floor buffer, driving the huge lawn mower, painting, laying floor tiles, and doing other light maintenance jobs. Starting pay was three dollars per hour, and $120 a week seemed like a fortune to the boys. Although Todd, who had started working a summer earlier, had seniority over Brian, Brian still called him by the nickname "Toddler."

The boys' crew chief was John Brabenec, who just happened to be dating Todd's older sister, Melissa. To avoid any show of favoritism, John constantly hassled Todd and Brian good-naturedly—especially about their crush on Mary Lou Retton, the gold-medal-winning Olympic gymnast who had been *Sports Illustrated*'s 1984 "Sportswoman of the Year." The boys pasted photos of the perky Retton all over the empty school while they did their custodial work—"for extra inspiration"—and even hatched a plan to travel to West Virginia in hopes of meeting Mary Lou. Their plan to meet the girl on the Wheaties box was dumped when the boys consulted a map and discovered just how far West Virginia is from Chicago. Since neither of them could drive yet, that was a long bike ride!

As long as Brian and Todd were doing a good job, Mr.

Greiff ignored the pictures of Mary Lou that had suddenly appeared around the school. He even allowed the boys to choose their own hours, expecting them to say, "Oh, let's work from 10 till 3." Normally Todd loved to sleep in whenever he could. But he loved to play basketball even more. So he and Brian reasoned, *If we start at 6:30 and get our work done early, we can play basketball the rest of the afternoon!* On many afternoons Mr. Greiff joined right in with them, as did the school's basketball coach, Steve Clum.

Coach Clum took a personal interest in all his players, and his influence on Todd was tremendous. Following Todd's eighth-grade season, Coach Clum wrote Todd a personal progress report:

> *You love the game. God has given you a tremendous ability to play basketball. Play for the Lord, and you will continue to experience success. Play with confidence. One of the finest athletes I've coached in nine years!*
>
> *Good court savvy. A quick, aggressive, unselfish player. Work on your left hand, because you might play guard in high school.*
>
> *Don't get down on yourself when things aren't going well. You're too good of a player to let that happen.*

Brian and Todd played together on the soccer team as well. But during their eighth-grade season, on the way to Todd's house one day, Brian flipped over the front of his bicycle, landing hard on the pavement and breaking his jaw. Out for the season, he was relegated to being the team's statistician. Todd, as a loyal friend, did his best to include Brian in the excitement of the game. Brian recalls, "Todd hung out with me on the sidelines when he wasn't off scoring two or three goals per game—which he often did. He made me feel that I was still part of the team."

Todd was a star soccer player, always right in the middle of the action. In one of the last games of the eighth-grade soccer season, Todd and an opponent came across the middle of the field. The opposing player attempted to "head" the ball but missed. His head slammed into Todd's jaw, literally pushing Todd's two front teeth back up inside his mouth. Todd reached up, pulled his teeth back down, and kept going! It was only when play was suspended that Todd realized his jaw was broken.

To facilitate the healing process, the doctor wired Todd's jaw shut. He could barely talk and could eat only foods that had been thoroughly liquefied in a blender. Yet, despite the liquid diet, Todd's appetite remained strong. He ate mashed potatoes and gravy—*really* mashed potatoes! He ate meat and lasagna, and even pizza, with a straw. Todd's jaw remained wired shut for six weeks, and he didn't lose a pound!

■ ■ ■ ■

Todd and Brian moved on to Wheaton Christian High School (known today as Wheaton Academy). There they added Keith Franz to their circle of friends. Keith had played for a rival grammar school, and Todd and Brian remembered him as a worthy adversary in basketball and soccer. Now they were happy to count him as a teammate.

Together the trio forged a friendship that would be known as "the three amigos" throughout high school. Even though Keith was the new kid on the block, he recalls, "I was cool because I hung out with Todd."

During their junior year, Keith was approached about running for class president. "I'm not going to do this unless one of you guys runs with me," Keith told Brian and Todd.

"Okay, dude," Todd replied. "You go for class president, and I'll run for vice president." It was a winning combination, and the Franz-Beamer ticket won by a landslide. But neither knew what he was getting into. Thinking that holding office would be fun, Todd and Keith quickly discovered they had been elected to serve rather than to be served.

One of their first responsibilities was to run the concession stand for the football games. One evening after soccer practice, Todd and Keith went to clean out the concession stand to get it ready for the season. They opened the door and couldn't believe their eyes. Apparently vandals had broken in to the building over the summer and sprayed a fire extinguisher everywhere—including in the hot-dog machine and the soda-pop coolers. Rats had moved in and made matters even worse! Dead rodents were strewn around the small room, and the food stand reeked with a pungent odor. The place was a mess! Todd took one look, glanced over at Keith, raised his eyebrows, and said, "Thanks, Franz. Being class officers is a real blast!"

Besides all his extracurricular activities, Todd was also a good student who always tried to get his work done ahead of schedule. Well organized and extremely disciplined, he didn't allow even his close friends to deter him from his studies. Keith often stopped by Todd's locker after school and found his friend loaded down with books and homework.

"What are you doing, taking the whole locker home?"

"Oh, I gotta study," said Todd.

"Come on, let's go have some fun," Keith cajoled.

"No, buddy, I've got to study," Todd stated emphatically.

And he did! He made mostly As and Bs throughout high school and had no trouble being accepted into college.

At the end of Todd's junior year in high school, the Beamers moved to Los Gatos, California, so David could move into a vice president's position with Amdahl at their corporate headquarters. It was a great opportunity for David, but Todd had to leave his Wheaton friends and spend his senior year in California. Todd desperately wanted to stay in Wheaton and devised plans to live with friends, but his parents felt it was important to keep the family together. So Todd decided to make the best of the move to California and jumped right in to school and sports. He tried out for the basketball team and, to no one's surprise, not only made the team but soon became the go-to guy at Los Gatos High School.

One reason Todd succeeded in sports was his natural ability. However, perhaps equally important, he was a "thinking" athlete. He kept his head in the game, no matter how great the pressure. He remained calm and rarely got flustered. He was often willing to risk doing something unconventional if it meant he might pull out a win.

For example, in one game he encountered a double-team, full-court press as he was trying to get the ball across center court. In a letter to his friend Keith, back in Wheaton, he described the situation. "Franz," Todd wrote, "they were hitting us with a full-court press. I was dribbling down the side, and two guys came over to double-team me. I looked across the lane and that guy was guarded. There was nowhere to go. I only had one option, so I went for it. I dribbled right through the defenders' legs! It was awesome!"

That was Todd. He always kept his cool.

Following graduation from high school, he enrolled in Fresno State as a physical therapy major. One night, during his first semester, he and some friends were driving home for the weekend. They had just gotten onto the freeway outside San Jose when a car roared up behind them and clipped the corner of their car. The driver of the vehicle in which Todd was riding lost control. The car careened off the road, flipped over, and then slammed into a ditch, trapping Todd and his friends inside the vehicle. Meanwhile, the driver who had caused the accident made no effort to stop. (Later Todd and his friends discovered that the hit-and-run driver had stolen the car and was making a getaway.)

Fortunately someone in another car following Todd's called for help. A rescue team arrived shortly and soon cut Todd and his friends out of the crunched automobile. Everyone in the car survived the crash, although one of Todd's friends suffered a broken back and had a long recovery. To Todd, the accident was a sign. Although he sustained only minor injuries, his bruises were enough to keep him from playing at his best during baseball season. After Todd failed to gain a spot on Fresno's Division I baseball team as a walk-on, Fresno lost its allure. He had been talking with Keith and Brian about transferring to Wheaton College, and the accident may have been the last straw.

A short time after that, Todd decided to return to Wheaton for the remainder of his schooling. He had started college anticipating a career in physical therapy. Then for a while he had chosen a premed major, thinking of becoming a doctor. Todd talked often with Rick Young, his Aunt Bonnie's husband, about the pros and cons of a career in medicine. After all, Uncle Rick was a successful radiologist who loved his work. Like Rick, Todd wanted to do something to help people. But Rick cautioned Todd about the long hours, the hassles of being on call, and the enormous expense involved in getting his education. "Medicine is changing," Rick told him. "In most cases you aren't able to develop relationships with patients, and the lifestyle can be costly to your family."

Todd weighed each factor carefully. "Yeah, you're right," he said slowly. "My heart's not really in medicine." That's when he decided to change his major at Wheaton College to business.

Todd wanted his life to count; he wanted to *live* the Christian life, not just talk about it. While many of Todd's college classmates went into ministerial professions, Todd felt that he didn't need to be a "professional" preacher to serve God. He could serve God in business as well—and maybe even make more of an impact on the world than he could by speaking from a pulpit. Although his close friends and family members didn't understand all that Todd meant at the time, one day they would . . . and in a way the go-to guy himself would never have guessed.

OUR PATHS
CROSS . . .

WHEN TODD MOVED from California back to Wheaton, Illinois, he transferred his school credits from Fresno State to Wheaton College. First he lived on the fourth floor of Traber Dorm with his longtime buddy Keith Franz. Two other lifelong friends of Todd's—Stan Ueland and John Schlamann—were right next door, and Brian Funck, his buddy since fifth grade, was just down the hall. The guys grandiosely referred to themselves as "The Men of Traber 4."

In later college years Todd moved into a four-man apartment on campus along with Keith and two other roommates: Dan Gunn and Rob Keyes during junior year; Dave Rockness and Todd Galde during senior year. Again, friend Stan Ueland lived next door.

While at Wheaton College, Todd was known for being mischievous, but never in a malicious sort of way. For instance, he had a strange habit of snacking on sardines. One day, after downing a can of the raunchy smelling fish,

Todd went into Stan and John's empty dorm room and placed the open can with the remaining oils on their heater. Todd then cranked the heat up high and closed the door. When Stan and John returned to their room, the foul fish smell had permeated the air, their bedding, their clothes—everything. The entire room reeked like a fishery!

Stan recalled later, "I didn't appreciate it at the time. But after the awful smell wore off, I had to admit it was one of those pranks I wished I'd thought of myself!"

Traber had community bathrooms and showers. Since the bathroom was a great gathering place for the guys every morning, it was also a frequent place for pranks. One of Keith and Todd's more devious tricks was to spray guys with cold water while they were in the shower. "Hey, real funny, Beamer," most guys would say. "I'm already wet."

Then, a second or two later, they'd realize: the cold-water concoction Keith and Todd had sprayed was made of water . . . and Bengay.

Another of Todd's favorite pranks was tossing firecrackers out the dorm window onto the sidewalk, just in front of one of his friends who was walking along. But no one ever thought of getting him in trouble. Todd was too well liked—and respected.

When Todd wasn't studying, he was on the basketball court or baseball field; he gave up soccer in college. Todd had a great deal of natural ability, but he also worked hard to develop his skills. He was extremely disciplined both on and off the practice field. He was known as a "gamer"—the guy who just wouldn't give up, who could be depended on to come through no matter the cost.

Once during a spring-break college baseball game in Florida, with his mom and dad in the stands, Todd came up to bat with Wheaton College behind in the game, two outs, bases loaded, in the last inning. Todd battled the pitcher to a 3 and 2 count. Every person in the bleachers was riveted to the field. The pitcher threw his best stuff, Todd swung evenly, and he blasted the ball out of the park for a grand slam!

Todd had an uncanny ability to pull off those kinds of things. During his last "at bat" of his college career, he belted the ball out of the park for a home run to win the game. He saved the ball and wrote on it, "Last college hit— solo shot." Yet even with all his successes, Todd never flaunted his abilities or accomplishments. He remained humble, a quality that endeared him to his friends and teammates.

Todd simply loved rooting for his beloved Chicago sports teams. He and his friends attended a lot of Chicago Cubs and White Sox games, sitting in the cheap seats at Wrigley Field or Comiskey Park and screaming their lungs out at the umpires (or anyone else who might be able to influence a Chicago victory). Occasionally they caught a Chicago Bulls game when they could scrounge some tickets. Todd was also a Chicago Bears fan and was especially proud of Walter "Sweetness" Payton, the Bears' sensational running back.

By far, though, Todd's favorite athlete was Chicago Bulls superstar Michael Jordan. Todd had followed Michael as a rising star at North Carolina and was thrilled when he was drafted by the Bulls. He admired Michael's amazing athleticism but also his uncanny ability to always make something exciting happen. Todd collected all kinds of Michael memorabilia to remind him of the success that follows fierce determination and a winning spirit.

While walking through the Wheaton train station one day, Todd spied a four-by-six-foot advertising poster that featured Michael Jordan on the court in his "work clothes," including the number 23 jersey that has since been retired by the Bulls organization. Todd was ecstatic. He'd worn Michael's number 23 on all his jerseys throughout high school and college.

"Oh, dude! That would look great in our apartment!" Todd told Keith. The next thing Keith knew, the poster was hanging on their living-room wall, opposite a huge American flag. "Hey, they were just going to throw it away," Todd explained when asked how he'd acquired the poster.

That poster became one of Todd's most prized possessions. After we were married, it traveled with us from home to home. In fact, it's still in our home today—although in our basement.

■ ■ ■ ■

On the first day of classes during the second semester of Todd's senior year, he attended the business department's Senior Seminar, a required course for all business and economics majors. That afternoon, following class, Todd burst through the door to his apartment. "Hey, Franz," he yelled to his roommate Keith. "Today I met the woman I'm going to marry!"

"Good joke," Keith answered skeptically, obviously unimpressed. "What's her name?"

"You know her. She's Paul Brosious's sister. Paul's on the baseball team with me."

"Isn't she practically engaged to some other guy?"

"Oh, don't say it!" Todd plopped down on the bed and clutched his stomach as though someone had punched him. "Don't tell me she's taken. She's perfect!" Then he rolled over and said tongue in cheek, "She should have waited. She doesn't know what she missed!"

Although I had no knowledge of it at the time, the woman Todd was raving about was . . . *me!*

I had known of Todd prior to that afternoon but hadn't interacted with him a great deal. I knew he was a good athlete, so I assumed he was the stereotypical jock—all hung up on himself as God's gift to women. He drove a cool car, too—a sporty black Honda Prelude. That only added to the jock image in my mind.

But through talking with my brother Paul, then a junior at Wheaton, and cheering him on during baseball games, I learned differently. Todd Beamer was the captain of Paul's team, an aggressive player and a good motivator who wasn't overbearing. Tall, good-looking, and quick to smile, he seemed to enjoy leading others, and he was the kind of man the other guys wanted to follow.

Paul had played baseball with Todd for two years and had nothing but good things to say about him. Although I'd heard all about Todd, I just never thought of him in a romantic sort of way.

Even on that first day of our Senior Seminar, our contact

was extremely limited. Todd came in and sat down in the
seat next to mine. He smiled casually; I noticed his red plaid
shirt and his relaxed manner. Before class began we talked
a bit about Paul and baseball. It was the first time we'd ever
spoken directly. Yet, despite our brief interaction, Todd
made an impression on me.

Because the class was a roundtable discussion group,
I had the opportunity to observe Todd as he interacted with
the other students. Soon I realized he was not at all the way
I had assumed. He was actually rather humble, soft-spoken,
bright, and articulate. I was particularly impressed by his
willingness to listen to the opinions of others and let them
take the lead in discussion. We became sort of partners in
the class, sharing ideas on projects and calling each other
about upcoming assignments.

Definitely impressed with Todd Beamer, I was a little
dismayed that I hadn't gotten to know him earlier in our
college years. I regarded our relationship as a budding
friendship. I wouldn't know until much later that Todd's
thoughts were more on the romantic side.

One day a few weeks into the Senior Seminar class, I
was chatting with my roommate, Kara Lundstrom. "Have
you ever met someone and found that they aren't at all like
you thought they were?" I asked.

"Who are you talking about?" Kara probed.

"Todd Beamer."

"Oh, yeah, I know Todd," she said. As an athletic trainer
on the basketball and baseball teams, Kara had worked
with Todd a lot. "I've known for a long time that he was a
good guy."

"Well, thanks for telling me!" I said with a laugh.

Then I let the matter drop. After all, I was dating someone else at the time. There was no place in my life for Todd Beamer . . . or so I thought.

I had no idea how many more conversations Kara and I would have about him in the years ahead.

A NORMAN
ROCKWELL WORLD

LITTLE DID I KNOW, at the time of Todd's and my first brief encounter in our Senior Seminar at Wheaton College, how much we would have in common . . . or that someday I, a girl from the hometown of Shrub Oak, New York, would become his wife.

Both of us grew up with parents who put a high value on family loyalty, faith in God, personal integrity, and a strong work ethic. My parents strongly encouraged a sense of family but also a spirit of independence. These may seem to be opposing values at first brush, but my mom and dad, Lorraine and Paul Brosious, modeled both qualities in such a manner as to make them complementary rather than contentious. No doubt my desire to have a close-knit family, as well as a meaningful career, was instilled in me by my parents' examples.

Lorraine Acker grew up in Sunbury, a rural, blue-collar community located in central Pennsylvania along the picturesque banks of the Susquehanna River. Paul Brosious lived just down the road, less than a mile from Lorraine, yet my future parents hardly knew each other until they were young adults.

Of German descent, Lorraine and her older brother, Ron, lived with their mom and dad right next door to their grandparents' home, so involvement with extended family was a concept ingrained in my mom. Having Grandma and Grandpa so close was like having an extra set of parents.

A community playground was located directly behind Lorraine's house, complete with a baseball field, basketball hoops, and a paid staff that organized activities for the kids all summer long. Lorraine loved sports. As a little girl, she often headed for the playground early in the morning and didn't return home until suppertime. But nobody worried. In Sunbury, everybody watched out for one another.

Lorraine's mom, Aletha, was a godly woman who desired to raise her children in the church. Her husband, Lawrence, loved nature and held strong conservative values. Yet, surprisingly—especially for that part of the country—he had no interest in having a relationship with God. Nor did he have any use for the church. He was an agnostic at best. In fact, he claimed to be an atheist, often ranting, "There is no God. I hate God!"—apparently oblivious to the contradiction in his statements.

Lorraine's family didn't own a car until she was 13 years old, so Aletha and the children walked to a nearby church every Sunday morning. That particular church excelled at educating children in Bible stories but put little emphasis on having a genuine relationship with God that could influence everyday life. So to Lorraine, the church seemed more like a social club than a place to gain faith that mattered. As a teenager, she participated in youth-group activities and even sang in the choir. But gradually the church became less and less relevant to her life. By the time she graduated from high school, she was ready to give up on religion altogether.

That summer, however, her brother, Ron, and his wife, Joyce, invited Lorraine to hear a speaker tell about how God had changed his life. There Lorraine heard and understood for the first time that Jesus loved her—and that he wanted to forgive her sins, encourage and guide her every day, and give her hope for the future with the promise of eternity in heaven. At the close of the service, the speaker asked if anyone wanted to commit their life to following Jesus. Ron leaned over and whispered in Lorraine's ear, "Do you want to make that decision? Would you like to go up front and pray?"

Reticent about making such a public expression of faith, Lorraine refused. Later that night, however, alone in her room, she took out a Bible and began to read. Before she closed the book, she had committed her life to God. Immediately she felt peace—and knew that God would be with her from then on. He would provide direction and purpose for her life. It finally made sense! God was not a character in a book. He was a real being who had created her and knew best what her life should look like. Even better, he loved her in a very personal way and was available for constant communication through prayer and reading his words in the Bible.

Upon hearing of Lorraine's decision, Joyce encouraged

her to attend a Bible college to learn more about who God was and how faith worked. "If you can get me in, I'll go," promised Lorraine. And she did! Although she had never been away from home before, within two weeks of her spiritual conversion she enrolled at a Bible school 1,200 miles from home. She bristled, however, at the school's legalistic convictions about the Christian life. To Lorraine, the emphasis seemed more on guilt than grace. Nevertheless, she felt that God had sent her there, so she stayed. The strong, cloistered Christian environment was a safe place to develop her fledgling faith, and she attended the school for two years before transferring back home to Susquehanna University.

Paul Brosious, her husband-to-be, was the youngest of seven children, raised with five brothers and one sister in a devout but poor Christian family. The family had little money because Paul's mother had been hospitalized several times during his childhood, and Paul's dad didn't make much as the groundskeeper of the local cemetery. Paul's older brothers—some of whom were old enough to be his father—pitched in together to help their dad eke out a meager living. Russell, one of the youngest, died fighting in the Pacific during World War II when Paul was seven years old. Paul was only nine years of age when his father died of a sudden illness. Older brother Earl stepped in to help his mom take care of Paul and their sister, Ruth.

About six feet tall, with an athletic build, Paul wasn't particularly debonair. But he was down-to-earth and easygoing—quick to smile and always ready to help anyone in need. A brilliant student, a self-starter, and highly motivated, Paul strove constantly to improve himself. Most of

Paul's siblings barely finished high school, let alone college, so it's not surprising that he received little encouragement to pursue higher education.

Consequently, he followed a vocational course in high school. He had a natural propensity for figuring out how mechanical things worked and could fix just about anything with moving parts. Upon graduating, Paul went to Washington, D.C., and took a course in radio technology. Then he returned to Sunbury and worked as a radio transmitter.

He was determined to go to college, so with nothing but a high school transcript—and that in a vocational program—Paul approached Susquehanna University. The university refused him. Next he tried Bucknell University and met with the same result. Finally he approached the admissions director at Bloomsburg State College (now Bloomsburg University) and, amazingly, Bloomsburg let him in!

Paul nearly failed his first college class, but a kindly professor recognized the student's potential and took him under his wing. For the remainder of his college career, Paul worked a 40-hour week while carrying a full load of classes at Bloomsburg . . . and graduated with highest honors.

Besides being extremely intelligent, Paul was the model of integrity, known for his honesty and impeccable morals.

Six years Lorraine's senior, Paul played on the church softball team with Lorraine's older brother. Because Ron thought Paul and Lorraine might be a good match, he made sure they had the opportunity to meet one Sunday after church. Before long Paul and Lorraine began dating and quickly fell in love. The following year they were married at the same church where they had met.

The young couple lived in Sunbury while Lorraine finished her college degree in English at Susquehanna. Meanwhile Paul taught physics in the local high school and earned his master's at Bucknell—the same school that had refused to admit him a few years earlier.

Next Lorraine and Paul moved to Philadelphia, where he began his Ph.D. work at the University of Pennsylvania. Dissatisfied with Penn, they moved to Albany, where Paul continued his doctoral studies at Albany State University. For the next six years Paul worked during the day and studied at night, until he had achieved his Ph.D. in physics. Then he remained on staff at Albany State University as a research physicist. That was Mom and Dad's primary source of income when I, the first of four children, was born on April 10, 1969.

My brother Paul came along the following year, and Holly was born four years later. Shortly after Holly's birth, Dad took a job as a research physicist with IBM, and we moved to Shrub Oak, just outside Peekskill and about half an hour north of New York City. After that, Mom and Dad must have needed a break, because our younger brother, Jonathan, wasn't born until I was 13 years old—nine years later!

■ ■ ■ ■

We had a Norman Rockwell type of upbringing, with Mom and Dad actively involved in our lives. Both Dad and Mom loved books. Dad preferred more technical, scientific reading, while Mom always had a new novel to explore. Rather than spending evenings plopped in front of a television set, many nights our family would play games or read books together. The Chronicles of Narnia by C. S. Lewis were family favorites, as well as the spiritual classic *Hinds' Feet on High Places* by Hannah Hurnard. We also enjoyed the Laura Ingalls Wilder books, so when we did watch television, our favorite show was *Little House on the Prairie.*

Indeed, we *were* an Ingalls sort of family in many ways. Mary Ingalls was a role model for me. Like me, she was the oldest sister in the family . . . the responsible one who got good grades and always watched out for her younger siblings. Laura was the younger one who naively got in trouble a lot, as did my brother Paul. Carrie, the younger, happy-go-lucky sister, reminded me of my sister, Holly.

Like any family, we had our occasional spats. But for the most part, our home was peaceful. However, when it got *too* quiet, Mom and Dad knew something was up and came to check on us. Once when Holly was only a baby and I was about five years old, Paul and I decided that our dog, Shep, a German shepherd, needed a haircut. Poor Shep never looked so bald!

We lived in a four-bedroom, ranch-style home on the edge of town, and Holly, Paul, and I each had our own bedroom. Good thing, too. My room was always extremely neat and organized, but Holly's looked like a tornado had blown through it. To this day the carpet in Holly's bedroom looks brand-new. That's because few people ever actually walked on it; her floor was usually covered with clothes, books, magazines, and who knows what else.

Holly and I collected miniature dollhouses, complete with tiny furniture and pictures on the wall. When Jonathan was a baby, he'd sometimes sneak into Holly's room and wreck her dollhouse furniture. That raised the roof! Somewhere, packed neatly away in a box in the basement, I still have my dollhouse. Holly's is still with us, too, although most of the contents are wrecked, thanks to Jonathan.

Our house had a large yard, which became the gathering place for all our friends. Whenever we were home from school, there was almost always something going on outside. We rode our bikes and played Wiffle ball, hide-and-seek, or games of PIG on the driveway basketball court. Even better, Mom and Dad played right along with us. They didn't care that the grass was being trampled; having fun together was far more important.

Inside, our home was a warm, loving environment, where Mom and Dad welcomed our friends day or night. It was the place kids wanted to be, where they felt comfortable. With three outgoing children and a toddler in the family, our home was always bustling. Mom made snacks for the constant parade of children, with no complaints. And not only that, she *always* tried to make things special. She threw the best "theme" birthday parties, and all our friends wanted to attend. She and Dad continually went out of their way to make our friends feel at home, and it worked!

From the time I was in fourth grade, one of my best friends was Janet Odland. She was the youngest sibling in her family; I was the oldest in mine. Janet was tall for our age and had long, dark hair; I was short and had short, blonde hair. But we were inseparable! When I wasn't at her house, Janet practically lived at our house. She'd hide in the closet when Dad was coming home, and he'd pretend he didn't know she was there. When Janet jumped out of her hiding place, Dad would feign surprise. "Oh, I can't believe you're here!" he'd say. "I'm so glad to see you!" Years later, Janet still remembered my dad's excitement over her presence in our home. "He always made me feel so special!" she told me.

Mom also headed up the Pioneer Girls group that met at our church. Similar to a Girl Scouts program, Pioneer Girls had award levels and all sorts of badges we could earn for accomplishing certain tasks. We proudly applied our merit badges to a sash that we wore at meetings and other special events. Pioneer Girls was a good experience for me. A type A person, even as a child, I was very goal oriented. Soon my sash was covered with badges.

Mom was an extremely creative leader, too. She was especially good at making inexpensive crafts such as corn-husk dolls, dried-apple doll heads, and a wide assortment of things from toilet-tissue rolls. Nowadays Mom and I laugh when we recall some of the crazy things we made from household scraps. "What were you thinking, Mom?" I tease her.

"I don't know what else we made," she says, smiling, "but we made some good memories."

That was all that mattered.

When I finished fifth grade, Mom talked my friend Janet and me into attending Pioneer Girls summer camp in the Adirondack Mountains. "You'll love it," Mom assured us.

As soon as we settled in to the camp, we knew we'd
been had. We hated it! We enjoyed the games and the
arts-and-crafts sessions, but the camp was extremely struc-
tured. It was run like a military outpost, complete with
a bugle playing reveille every morning at seven o'clock.

I was used to the camping routine since I'd camped
with my family from the time I could walk. But Janet had
never been camping anywhere. We signed up for an activity called "Wilderness Exploration," and part of the trip
involved wading through a swamp up to our elbows. That
ended Janet's interest in camping.

In contrast, my family loved to go camping in Cape
Cod, Massachusetts, or in New York's Adirondack Mountains. We roughed it out in the wild country, cooked our
meals over an open campfire, and slept under the stars
or in a tent. At night, we'd sit around the campfire and
talk—about funny things and serious things. We'd tell
silly stories and occasionally even a few ghost stories. But
mostly it was just family talk and a special time to be
together.

The older I got, the less I enjoyed camping—mainly
because I missed the finer things in life, like electricity,
running water, a warm shower, a telephone, and a hair
dryer! But I didn't usually mind camping . . . until it
rained.

One time I had just snuggled into my sleeping bag in
our tent after an exhilarating day of hiking through the
mountains, topped off by one of Mom's open-flame-cooked
meals and a good time of conversation around the campfire
after dinner. Just as I was drifting off to sleep, I heard the

first drops of rain spattering on the roof of the tent. I didn't think anything of it until I awoke later to find a small river running through my sleeping bag!

■ ■ ■ ■

Sports played a major role in my family just as they did in Todd's—especially for Paul, but for Holly, Jonathan, and me, too. I loved playing basketball and soccer. Mom coached the community girls' softball team, so naturally I played on that, too.

At least once a year, Mom and Dad took us to Yankee Stadium to see a Major League Baseball game. That was always a highlight of our summer. We packed a lunch and cheered enthusiastically for our favorite players. Since Paul and Holly were both avid New York Yankees fans, I became one by default.

Collecting baseball cards was a popular activity around our house, and in elementary school, I'd often "flip" baseball cards with the boys. The winner of the flip got to keep the cards. After winning, I'd race home to show Paul the new cards I'd won from the boys that day. Paul was proud to have a sister who knew her baseball cards!

Even our pets were named after sports figures—Matty, the dog, after Yankees star Don Mattingly; and Emmy, the cat, after Emmitt Smith of the Dallas Cowboys. Although we had an assortment of pets as I was growing up, my favorite was a black-and-white runt kitten named Willie, after Billy "White Shoes" Johnson, a football player who wore white shoes as his signature. My dad suggested the name when he saw Willie's white feet.

Willie was born to our family cat, Tatsy, who had been hiding in my bedroom closet prior to giving birth. I was in third grade at the time. Imagine my surprise when I opened the closet and found Tatsy giving birth to what looked to me like frogs! My parents assured me they would be cute, fluffy kittens soon, and of course they were. The smallest was Willie, and I immediately fell in love with him. He became my baby. I dressed him in my dolls' clothes, placed him in a stroller, and pushed him all around the neighborhood.

One day Willie decided to take a little trip. When he didn't come back by nightfall, I was worried sick. He was gone for 10 full days, and I was devastated. I prayed for his safe return but was convinced he'd died. Then one morning while I was eating breakfast, Mom called to me from the front door. "Lisa, come here!"

I ran to the door and there was Willie, sitting on the steps, looking at me as if to say, *Well, what's your problem? You should have known I'd be back!*

Although I never found out where Willie had gone, I was thrilled he had come home to me. And I realized that sometimes miracles really *do* happen. Willie was my loyal friend from third grade right up to the time I went to college. It was hard to leave him behind!

But even harder was the pain of losing our much-loved childhood pets when they died. Brutus, one of our dogs, died when Paul and I were attending Wheaton College. Mom called me first because she knew Brutus's death would be especially hard on Paul. She thought it might be better if I broke the news to him in person. Ironically, Willie also died while we were at Wheaton, and Paul had to break the news to me.

■ ■ ■ ■

My family stayed involved in a variety of activities. For instance, my younger sister, Holly, and I were part of the student government in our high school, while Paul kept busy with sports. We also enjoyed music, and we all took piano lessons. I stayed with it longer than my brothers and sister, but none of us were really good musicians. Holly and I both played the flute in band. Dad was a good singer, having once sung in a gospel quartet. He taught himself to play harmonica, and he could plunk out a few tunes on the piano as well, so I guess what little musical ability I inherited came from him. In the years to come, Todd's and my lack of musical ability would be a running joke with our friends.

Through my entire growing-up life, the Peekskill Baptist Church was a focal point; many of our family activities revolved around it. Mom and Dad were leaders in the church. Similar to Todd's family, our parents didn't consider church attendance optional; it was expected. Even in our teenage years, we never resisted going to church or debated about its merits. We always prayed at mealtimes and often had devotional readings after dinner. When tucking us into bed, Mom or Dad always paused long enough to talk with each of us privately for a few minutes and to pray with us individually before kissing us good night.

When I was seven, I prayed and told Jesus I wanted to commit my life to following him. However, since I was so young, I didn't know all that decision meant until later. My realization expanded as I grew up. I didn't have a crisis experience or a dramatic turnaround. Instead, my relationship with God evolved naturally. God was always a part of my life. I didn't have to work up my faith or manufacture some outrageous testimony. I learned early on that God loved me, and I believed that as I trusted him with my life, he'd take care of me.

■　■　■　■

Holidays were special times around our house, especially Thanksgiving and Christmas. We always had a touch football game out in the yard before dinner. After the game, we cleaned up and prepared for one of Mom's delicious home-cooked meals, complete with turkey, mashed potatoes, and stuffing. At Thanksgiving dinner, Mom had a tradition of placing dried kernels of corn on each plate. The number of kernels represented the number of things we had to say we were thankful for. We didn't often verbalize our appreciation for each other or for those things that each of us treasured, so the Thanksgiving tradition provided a good opportunity. It was always a special time as each of us around the table, including Mom and Dad, expressed our gratitude to God and to each other. "I'm thankful I finally have a cat of my own," Holly would say shyly. "I'm thankful for my brothers and sister," I'd offer with a smile for each. "I'm thankful I can play baseball," Paul would say seriously.

Sometimes, after a big Thanksgiving dinner, the entire family worked off the meal by hiking up Turkey Mountain, a nearby peak overlooking the Croton Reservoir. If the weather was just right, on a clear day we could see all the way to the New York City skyline, with the Empire State Building and the World Trade Center towers clearly in sight. The day after Thanksgiving, we went as a family and chopped down our Christmas tree.

Independence, patriotism, freedom, and the American way of life were not trite clichés tossed around lightly in our family. They were highly treasured values. Both Dad and Mom had relatives who had died in World War II, so we always displayed a flag in front of our house on Memorial Day, Flag Day, Independence Day, and Veterans Day. We often celebrated the Fourth of July with our extended family in Pennsylvania and then returned with a load of firecrackers, which we loved to set off in our driveway.

■ ■ ■ ■

As the oldest child, I was paving the way for my brothers and sister, so everything I wanted to do was a big deal. It was a major issue when I wanted to attend my first middle-school dance as an eighth grader. Dad was extremely protective, especially of his daughters. Moreover, growing up he'd been taught that dancing wasn't something good kids did. So it wasn't surprising his response to my request to go to the dance was a categorical "No!"

Crushed, I appealed to Mom. Mom and Dad rarely disagreed on parenting issues, but in this case, she sided with me. She didn't see any harm in dancing and trusted me to use good judgment. She knew that as we became teenagers, there would be many times she and Dad would have to give us a little freedom and have faith that we would use it wisely.

Dad finally acquiesced, and I had a good time at the dance. He was still waiting up for me when I got home, though.

I've always appreciated Mom's going to bat for me on that one. Had my parents attempted to keep me reined in by the same legalistic rules that they had endured, it's quite possible I might have rebelled. I was far too independent to abide by those rules for long. Besides, Mom and Dad needn't have worried; I was tougher on myself than they were!

I was a good student with almost straight As on my report card. Math, science, and American history were my favorite subjects, and I was conscientious to a fault. I started worrying about taking my SATs when I was a freshman in high school!

Because of my family's German ethnic background, I elected to take German as my foreign language requirement in school. As a "fringe benefit," I was invited to travel to Germany as an exchange student and live with a German family for a full month. I was barely 15 years old and had never been away from my family except to go to camp. I had hardly traveled out of the state and had never been on an airplane. But early in August that year, I boldly waved good-bye to Mom and Dad and boarded the bus taking the group of exchange students from our school in Shrub Oak to New York's Kennedy Airport. Traveling on my own was an entirely new experience for me, a well from which I would draw deeply in the years to come.

While overseas I lived with the Frey family, whose daughter Sabina was my age. Sabina showed me around her high school and introduced me to her friends. Although I was studying German, I wasn't fluent in the language, so for the next four weeks I communicated mostly by hand motions and facial expressions. I was horribly homesick, but there was no way I was going to admit that to anyone!

The Frey family treated me wonderfully. Sabina's father was a banker, and the family owned a chalet in Switzerland and a second home in Paris. Each weekend I was there we traveled to another part of Europe, expanding my horizons even further.

I was struck by the immense cultural differences I observed between life in Germany and life in America. For instance, in my community, teenagers weren't supposed to drink alcohol. But in Germany, kids my age drank regularly. After school, Sabina and her friends usually stopped by the bar for a few beers before doing their homework. I was shocked! Families in Germany made a common practice of sharing a large meal together in the middle of the day, while in Shrub Oak, many families struggled even to have dinner at the same table. Kids in America expected parents to drive them wherever they wanted to go, but kids in Germany hopped on a bus or train on their own. Most families I knew at home professed some kind of faith and many regularly attended church or synagogue. In Germany

God wasn't mentioned much, and I didn't see anyone go to church.

Although I appreciated the chance to see a whole different way of life, I was thrilled to get back to the U.S. Never had the flag meant so much to me as when I saw it flying over our school when we returned in early September 1984.

In October Sabina came to spend a month with my family in New York. Unfortunately, my family never got the opportunity to return the kindness Sabina's family had extended to me. Little did I know, as Mom and Dad welcomed me back home, that our Norman Rockwell world was about to change forever.

6

WRESTLING WITH THE "WHYS"

SOME TEENAGERS tend to rebel—whether outwardly or inwardly—against their parents during their junior high and high school years. They allow peer pressure, raging hormones, or other things to drive a wedge between themselves and the people who love them the most. For some reason, by age 15, that hadn't happened to me. I loved my parents and had a good relationship with them; I admired my mom and adored my dad.

Although I didn't always agree with Mom and Dad's rules, I never doubted for a moment that they loved me and wanted the best for me. We teased each other and often engaged in good-natured horseplay. Dad loved to interact with my teenage friends, too. My good friend Janet especially loved to hear his scientific explanations. When she was at our house for dinner, she'd ask Dad such imponderable questions as "When I put my plate in the microwave, why does my food get hot but my plate doesn't?" Then she'd sit back and smile as my dad launched into a long, drawn-out explanation. My friends all thought Dad was funny; I just thought he was embarrassing! But I loved him nonetheless.

Dad brought incredible stability to our family. He was a strong leader, yet very tender and loving. He didn't have to flex his muscles, raise his voice, or do anything to show that he was in charge; his very presence elicited peace, calm, and security.

Dad strove to balance his career and family responsibilities. No matter how busy he was or what stress and pressure he was under at work, he always made time for us. He made it a point to be home for dinner almost every night, and he rarely traveled for business so he could be available to Mom and us kids. As best he could, he worked his schedule around ours to avoid missing even one of our school programs, birthday parties, ball games, or other special events in our lives. Dad was always there for us.

One of the best things he did for us was to love Mom. He showed her respect, asked her opinions, encouraged her pursuits, and laughed with her. He greeted her with hugs and kisses when he came in the door every night. We saw not only their arguments but also how they resolved those differences. No matter what else was wrong in the world, I was sure my parents would always be together. There was tremendous security in our family. Mom and Dad weren't bashful about letting us know that they were still in love, even after nearly 18 years of marriage and four kids!

Dad was a devout man, and his faith was a reasoned,

scientific approach to Christianity rather than an emotion-oriented faith. As a research physicist, he analyzed everything, and I loved to hear him explain biblical truths and why he believed them. He was on the deacon board at church, which meant he helped the pastor serve the congregation and run the business of the church. He also led Boys' Brigade, the male counterpart of the Pioneer Girls program.

Most of all, Dad was a man of unquestionable integrity. His life consistently matched his words. What people saw in him outside the home was exactly the sort of person he was inside the home.

Dad could fix anything. No matter what broke—my bicycle, the plumbing, or even a car engine—I never worried. *Daddy will fix it*, I'd tell myself. *As long as Daddy is here, everything is okay.*

One evening in late October 1984, following my return from Germany, I passed Dad in the upstairs hallway outside my room. I purposely bumped into him, and we jokingly jostled one another.

"Hey, watch that stuff!" Dad pretended to be hurt and offended.

I giggled and shoved on by him.

Dad appeared to be the picture of health as he bounded down the stairs.

Amazingly, he seemed to have escaped the health problems that plagued his siblings. We had already attended the funerals of several of our uncles. When I was 14, one of Dad's older brothers suffered an aneurysm; he survived that crisis but died of cancer a short time afterward. Two other brothers died of heart problems. All of Dad's brothers died in their fifties.

But we never dreamed *our* dad would have any health problems.

Dad ate a healthy, balanced diet, was physically active, and never seemed stressed about anything. He had coached Paul's baseball team that summer and, now that fall had arrived in New York, enjoyed playing touch football with our family and Sabina, the German exchange student who had come to live with us for the month.

On Thursday morning, October 25, Dad went to work. Suddenly, with no previous warning signs or indications that something might be wrong, immobilizing pains seared through his chest. His coworkers thought he was having a heart attack.

He was rushed to the local hospital, but his condition was misdiagnosed; the doctors simply ran tests and kept him overnight for observation. When I got home from school, Mom told Paul, Holly, and me that Dad was in the hospital because he had been having chest pains, but he seemed to be okay. I was worried sick, but Mom appeared confident that Dad's condition was stable, so her attitude buoyed my confidence. That night Mom went back to the hospital, and I stayed home with my brothers and sister. As the oldest of the four children, I felt I needed to be strong for everyone else.

The next morning at 5:00 A.M., the doctor called Mom to tell her that Dad had suffered an aortic aneurysm. A small hole had developed in the wall of his aorta, which was preventing adequate blood supply to his heart. The hole had to be repaired immediately to prevent a complete stoppage of blood to the heart. "We can't do anything more for him here. We need to move him to another hospital to do the surgery because we don't have the proper equipment," the doctor concluded.

Before she headed to the hospital, Mom woke us up so we could get ready for school. Then, by my bedside, Mom explained to Paul, Holly, and me that the hospital had called and the doctors were going to do emergency surgery. "They're going to move Daddy to another hospital," Mom said. "We need to pray." At about 6:30 A.M. we were in the process of praying when the phone rang again. Mom left the room to answer it. When she came back, she blurted through her tears, "They tried to move Dad, but it was too late. He died."

At first we were all stunned to silence. Then the tears began to flow.

I had no last opportunity to see my dad's smile, to hug him one more time, to tell him I loved him, or to say good-bye.

In that instant my world fell apart. I wasn't ready for this. I was 15 years old and just beginning to wrestle with a lot of life's tough questions. I felt cheated. Dad was our foundation, the rock we all depended on. He not only provided for our family financially, but his mere presence in our home also provided an incredible sense of security. Now he had been ripped out of our lives! And suddenly what was "always all right" as long as Daddy was here had gone terribly wrong.

What were we going to do? I was scared, hurt, and

angry—all at the same time. I railed at God, sometimes overtly, but most of the time expressing a silent rage. *God, you could have prevented this tragedy if you had wanted to! Why didn't you?* I would cry inwardly. *Don't you love us? This isn't the way things are supposed to be!*

My faith in God was severely shaken. Questions pummeled my heart and mind. *Why, God? Why did you allow this to happen? Why did you allow our father to be snatched away in the prime of life? You're supposed to be a good God. Dad was a good man; he was serving you the best he knew how. I still believe in you, but this just doesn't seem fair! Everyone else still has a dad.*

Yesterday, life had been wonderful. Our family was intact, and I had dreams for a fabulous future, certain to be fulfilled. Now, virtually overnight, life itself became uncertain. I had never felt so vulnerable. The void from Dad's unexpected death seemed impossible to fill.

■ ■ ■ ■

The next few days were a blur as Mom grappled with the myriad details involved when someone dies unexpectedly. Funeral and burial arrangements, relatives traveling in from other states, not to mention the matters of basic sustenance—all threatened to overwhelm us. Making matters worse, Mom learned from a friend at the hospital that ineptitude or malpractice might have led to Dad's death. If the doctors had properly diagnosed the condition 24 hours earlier, they would have had time to complete the surgery before the aorta tore open. In the months to come, Mom's friends advised her to bring a lawsuit against the hospital, which she eventually did. The lawsuit would drag on for seven years.

Many people in the church rallied around Mom to help. Others offered pious platitudes about it being Dad's time to go and how God must have needed him in heaven more than we did on earth. Some of our Christian friends and family members wanted to put a "happy face" on everything.

Mom smiled kindly at their sentiments, but that didn't change the fact that Dad was gone—that her children were without a father and she was without her husband. Glib answers from well-meaning people were simply unacceptable to her. Yes, we had our faith and believed solidly that God had everything under his control, but the hole in our family was real.

■ ■ ■ ■

Following Dad's death, we continued to attend church and youth-group activities. In fact, the weekend following the funeral, we were already back in church. But I retreated into a less visible role. Paul and I, in particular, struggled with our faith. Although Mom encouraged us to talk about Dad's death, both Paul and I were reluctant. Paul questioned, "Why did God allow Dad to die? I don't understand. Dad honored his parents, and the Bible says that if we honor our parents our lives will be long on the earth. It's not fair."

After Dad's death, Paul's grades dropped like a rock. And sports, which he had always loved, became his life.

Mom tried to help us talk about our feelings. She even

took us to a local counselor, hoping we might open up more. But for me, the pain and confusion were too intense to share with anyone. Nothing anyone said seemed to make me feel better, so I kept my thoughts and emotions to myself.

Because my struggle was more internal, Mom didn't know until much later that I too was grappling with my faith. She could tell I was sad, and she noticed the difference in my attitude. But life for most 15-year-old girls is rather tumultuous, so she didn't see any need to be alarmed. I kept my grades up and maintained an exterior image that everything was okay. But inside I was seething. I had always tried to do what was right; now I decided I had been duped by God. Although I never got to the point where I wanted to dump the whole God thing and I didn't go wild or become a "bad" person, I definitely stopped caring about who God wanted me to be and focused more on what I wanted to do. I was angry at God. "You really messed up here, God," I told him point-blank. I still hung out with the honor-roll type of kids, but my attitude had soured.

My brother Paul could sense the shift in my attitude. He recognized I was slipping away from my faith and edging ever closer to danger. Occasionally he'd try to bring me to my senses, gently nudging me back on the right path. "Lisa, what are you doing?" he'd ask. "This isn't the person you want to be."

Throughout my teenage years, Dad's death cast long shadows over my beliefs. I continued to wrestle with the "why" questions that often came calling when I least expected them . . . at night, just as I was about to drift off to sleep. As I longed for Dad's comforting voice, his faith-filled prayers, and his soft kiss on my forehead, I'd whisper, "Why?"

Why did God allow it to happen?

Why was the hospital not able to recognize Dad's problem?

Why didn't God protect our family from this evil?

Why *our* family?

And why now?

When I look back at this time of my life, what surprises me is that, even in the middle of those deep questions, I didn't once question God's existence . . . even if I couldn't understand his ways. Instead, most of my questions landed back in God's lap, as I gazed up at my heavenly Father with naive but genuine faith and asked, "Why, God?" I couldn't understand God's seeming indifference to my dad's death or our family's suffering.

Every person who has ever grieved the loss of a loved one has known that awful feeling. Despite our faith, sometimes life just hurts. God didn't answer my "why" questions, but he did confirm a message to me through the Bible. Over and over I was reminded of a promise God made through the prophet Jeremiah: *"For I know the plans I have for you," declares the Lord, "plans to prosper you and not to harm you, plans to give you hope and a future"* (Jeremiah 29:11). Although I didn't understand the full ramifications of those words, they provided a candle of light to help me through an extremely dark passageway in my life.

Eventually I came to realize that God knew what was going to happen to my dad. He knew the difficult circumstances my family would face and yet, for some reason I still can't comprehend, he chose not to change the course of events.

Slowly I began to understand that the plans God has for us don't just include "good" things, but the whole array of human events. The "prospering" he talks about in the book of Jeremiah is often the outcome of a "bad" event. I remember my mom saying that many people look for miracles—things that in their human minds "fix" a difficult situation. Many miracles, however, are not a change to the normal course of human events; they're found in God's ability and desire to sustain and nurture people through even the worst situations. Somewhere along the way, I stopped demanding that God fix the problems in my life and started to be thankful for his presence as I endured them.

Meanwhile, in the midst of her own pain, Mom stepped up and did her best to maintain some sense of normalcy in our lives. She didn't have hours to sit and cry; she had four kids to care for. Consequently, she didn't take a lot of time to grieve; she plunged right back into the daily grind. Years later she admitted, "I'm not sure I handled it in the best way." But at the time, that was the only choice that made any sense to her.

When Mom did show her grief, I cringed. I hated to see her hurting, and I tried to ignore her pain. It was too difficult for me to bear my own grief and empathize with Mom at the same time. We got to the place where we hid our pain from each other, but it was always there, right below the surface.

Ever the skeptic, my grandfather thought Dad's death would finally convince my mom that "her religious beliefs" were foolish and that Christianity was a sham. Just the opposite happened. Mom dug in even deeper, depending on God for her very existence.

Her attitude was, *I hate this, but I don't want to waste this. I really want to learn what I'm supposed to get out of this. When a father leaves behind little children and a wife, it's not a good thing. It's evil. But God can turn the evil to good.* A part of the Bible that was particularly meaningful to her was the account of Joseph, one of her favorite Old Testament characters. Years after Joseph's jealous brothers left him to die in a pit and then sold him into slavery, Joseph became the second-most powerful man in Egypt. When his brothers discovered that Joseph was now in charge of the food supply—and this during a severe famine—they feared for their lives. But when Joseph confronted them about what they had done to him earlier, he told them, "You meant it for evil, but God meant it for good, that many people would be saved."[1]

"This life isn't all there is," Mom repeatedly told us kids. "It's merely a drop in the bucket. We're here to prepare ourselves for eternity and to help other people do the same. Life isn't easy, but the good news is that, even at its best, it can't compare to how great heaven is going to be."

Mom didn't overspiritualize our problems, but she did try to keep the big picture in our minds. God had an ultimate plan for our eternity, but he was also interested in taking care of us here and now. He gave us help in so many ways and through many people. One of these was Joe Urbanowicz, a volunteer youth-group leader at our

[1]See Genesis 50:20

church, who came to our house day after day, night after night, to spend time with our family. In his early thirties, Joe worked for the school district. He and his wife, Karen, didn't have children of their own at the time, so they "adopted" us.

A big man of Polish descent, Joe had a full head of medium brown hair and a thick beard. An athletic guy, he'd played with my dad on the church softball team. Karen had been my second-grade Sunday school teacher and was still working in the church, along with Joe, as a youth leader when I became a teenager.

When Dad died, Joe told us, "I'm going to have an important role in your lives; I'm going to be here for you." And he always was. Joe and Karen were also a wonderful example of what a Christian marriage could be. Their love for each other spilled over to everyone else. Even after they had children of their own, Joe and Karen continued to be involved in our lives.

Sometimes, after a long day's work, Joe would come over to our place to play catch with Paul or to chat with Holly and me. Inevitably, the conversation turned to spiritual issues, as Joe helped me to understand more of what it meant to have a relationship with God. Occasionally we'd talk about my "why" questions, but Joe never made me feel foolish for asking. Nor did he ever condemn me for expressing my doubts. He didn't always tell me what I wanted to hear, but I knew he'd always shoot straight with me. Although he wasn't shy about giving advice, he was also a good listener. And most of all, I could tell he really cared. Joe never expected pats on the back or sought accolades. He simply saw a need and stepped in to meet it. Today Joe and Karen are still the youth leaders in the church where I grew up.

Another person who gave me direction in the years following my dad's death was Jim Daniels. The owner of a building-supply business in our area, he taught my Sunday school class. He also taught me to drive stick shift, ignoring the gears I stripped on his car! Later he discussed college options with me, encouraged me to consider a business major, and helped with my college application process. He even wrote recommendations and traveled with me on some college visits.

I had considered several schools and knew I wanted to go to a liberal arts college—probably one that would allow me to explore my faith as well as challenge me academically. I'd visited a few colleges on the East Coast, but nothing felt quite right. My friend Gigi Kemp and my cousin Matt Acker were students at Wheaton College, a well-known Christian liberal arts college in the Chicago suburbs. Although I hadn't wanted to go so far from home, I decided to check out Wheaton because Gigi's and Matt's enthusiasm for the school was contagious. During the fall of my senior year, Jim Daniels and his wife, Paula, were to attend a conference in the Chicago area; they invited me to travel with them to visit the Wheaton campus.

As soon as I stepped on campus at Wheaton, I knew. *This is it! This is how a college campus is supposed to look,* I thought, impressed with the old, stately buildings with ivy growing up the exterior stone walls. I liked the people I met there as well and felt sure that Wheaton would be a good fit for me. In fact, I was so certain Wheaton was the place for me that I didn't even apply at any other school. It was almost as if God was directing me there.

■ ■ ■ ■

After my father's death, finances were a challenge for our family. IBM provided a small pension, but it wasn't enough to raise four children and put them through college. Mom knew she'd need to begin working. She wanted to do something that would allow her to make a decent income while still spending adequate time with us, especially Jonathan, until we were out of school. So Mom went back to her teaching roots for a while, tutoring high school students, teaching preschool, and working on her master's in education. Eventually she decided to use the wisdom she'd gained in her life to help others through difficult problems, so she went back to school to become a counselor. She earned her master's in counseling and started her own counseling center at our church in Peekskill, a practice she continues today.

Watching Mom deal with the financial stress created by Dad's untimely death left an indelible impression on me. I told myself, *I never want to be in that vulnerable position.* My parents weren't financially irresponsible; they worked hard, made good money, and were extremely frugal. But no one ever counseled them on the need for sufficient life insurance. That was a mistake I vowed never to make. I knew firsthand how unexpected life's events can be. I wanted to hope for the best but plan for the worst.

Despite tenuous finances, Mom vowed that each of us would go to college and emerge debt-free. She and Dad had placed a premium on education and believed that a college degree would be their final gift in enabling us to build our own independent lives. So they had begun saving for our college while we were still toddlers. Many years later, I know she was proud to see each of us graduate and begin to make our own way in the world. We were so thankful to her, too, for the sacrifices she'd made to get us there.

Those years after my dad's death were not easy. But through all the pain, each of my family members grew stronger. We developed a depth of character. Paul became more compassionate, wanting to help kids make good choices and get the best start possible. Today he is a school psychologist. Holly challenged herself to make a difference, even if only in one or two individuals' lives; today she works with autistic children. Jonathan was only two when Dad died, so his grief has been more of a gradual process. He experienced the loss over a period of years as he discovered what he missed by never really knowing our dad. Today he's in college, considering a career in business. He has a wonderful ability to empathize with people and is a great influence wherever he goes.

As for me, I became much more independent. As I grew older, I made a subconscious pact with myself to always be sure I could take care of myself and my responsibilities. Although too much self-sufficiency can be bad—if it leads you away from God and into selfishness or delusion—my determination wasn't a prideful thing. I simply realized, because of my dad's death, that I needed to do as much as possible to prepare for the practical side of life while still appreciating God as the ultimate provider and relying on his direction.

More than anything, experiencing the array of emotions common to grief and working through the "why" questions pertaining to my faith in God was an important time of learning for me. I'd never have guessed it was also a time of preparation.

7

STEPPING OUT
ON FAITH

I COULDN'T WAIT to turn 16. Mom had promised she
would teach me to drive, and I was counting the hours. My
youth-group leader Joe Urbanowicz teased me incessantly,
saying things such as, "I just heard on the news that the
state is raising the driver's age to 18." Of course, the state
was doing no such thing, but I wasn't taking any chances.

On my 16th birthday, Mom took me to the Department
of Motor Vehicles to get my learner's permit. I drove all the
way home in our old brown Ford Fairmont station wagon.
Something about having my driver's license represented
freedom and autonomy; it was an important rite of passage
for me. Paul and I had to share the car, but since he's a year
younger than I am, I got first dibs on the car during my
junior year of high school.

Driving and dating were two of my favorite activities
during the last two years of high school. Where conversations with my friend Janet used to revolve around how
to decorate our dollhouses, now they focused on our

boyfriends—or potential boyfriends. Janet had a steady boyfriend throughout high school, but I never dated the same guy for more than a few weeks. If I detected a flaw in a fellow's personality or character, it was bye-bye! Since a friend and I kept the statistics for my brother Paul's baseball team, it wasn't surprising that many of my high school dates were with athletes. But none of those guys kept my interest for long. Sometimes it worried me that I wanted to break up with a guy after only a few weeks of dating him. I didn't want to be picky, but on the other hand, I would rather be on my own than with a guy who didn't seem right for me. I didn't want to settle for less than the ideal.

I wasn't sure I'd ever find my ideal guy, but I knew that college would afford me an opportunity to at least expand the possibilities. The college search wasn't a difficult one for me. I had grown up in a public school, and I was longing for an environment where I could relax and grow in my Christian faith—a place like Wheaton College. I was tired of constantly facing the decision of whether to compromise what I believed or fight for my faith. I didn't want to live in a sheltered, sequestered environment for the rest of my life, but the thought of doing so for a season seemed quite attractive.

Like most college students, I was a little nervous about moving away from home for the first time. But it was really harder on Mom than on me. As Mom drove her car away from my dormitory, my roommate, Kara Lundstrom, and I watched out the window, waving at her cheerfully. I was apprehensive, but I knew Mom was probably fighting back the tears.

Mom didn't really want me to work during my first year in college. She said, "I want you to enjoy your time in school." But I wanted to work, so I got a job as a part-time nanny, watching the daughter of a family that lived near the college. Both parents worked outside the home, so my responsibility was to pick up their young daughter after school and stay with her until the mom and dad got home from work. As a perk, the family allowed me to use one of their cars, a Buick Century. That was a godsend because I couldn't afford a car of my own at the time. I worked for that family all four years of college, and the extra money came in handy.

I planned on becoming a doctor, so I enrolled in the premed curriculum. Although I was extremely career oriented, I also hoped to have a family someday. When I took an economics class and liked it, I decided to switch my major to business. No one else in my family had studied business, but it seemed like a field that might offer more flexibility than the medical profession. I couldn't possibly have imagined at the time that a switch in my major might have such a profound effect on my life.

Switching majors, however, didn't diminish my growing desire to help hurting people. I just sought out different ways of doing so. One way came as a surprise.

Every summer Wheaton College sends some students out to various parts of the world to offer practical assistance with food, housing, and medical needs, while attempting to help people in other countries understand that God loves them. When I first heard about the short-term opportunity, my initial response was, "I could never do that!" I've always had a great respect for people who pack up and move to a foreign culture to share God's love there. Growing up, I got the impression that if I was really going to be a good Christian, I should train to be in some sort of formal, "professional" ministry.

But at Wheaton College, I came to realize that true Christians follow Jesus' example of compassion all the time, whether in full-time Christian service, working in a department store, waiting tables in a restaurant, or cranking out multimillion-dollar deals on Wall Street. Whether you're helping to pull starving, homeless people out of the ditches of Calcutta, visiting the elderly at a nursing home, or teaching inner-city kids to read, if you are doing what Jesus would do, acting the way Jesus would act, and showing his love to others, you are doing "ministry."

Nevertheless, I felt I needed to at least make myself available to go on the missions trip. I regarded it as a challenge I should take to prove to myself that I could do it, while opening myself to whatever God might want to show me through the experience. So I interviewed for the program during my sophomore year. Just before I went home for Thanksgiving break, I received word that I'd been accepted to serve in Indonesia.

"Indonesia? Where in the world is Indonesia?" I asked.

A friend got out a globe and pointed out a tiny country . . . on the opposite side of the earth from Wheaton, Illinois. "Here it is!" she said blithely. "Here's where you're going to spend your summer." I had no idea what to expect.

Throughout the academic year, we prepared for our trip. A student who had gone on a previous missions trip to the exact location where I'd be working tried to help by emphasizing the importance of getting all my shots before traveling. He filled my mind with horror stories of how he'd lived in the jungle and contracted all sorts of diseases. He told me awful tales about bugs, leeches, and worms, and every story made my flesh crawl. I've always been deathly afraid of snakes, and I started imagining huge reptiles chasing me through the jungles of Indonesia. I wasn't even sure that Indonesia had any jungles, but if they did, I just knew they'd be filled with snakes all slithering after me! *What am I doing going on this trip?* I wailed to myself.

But then I came to the place where I realized, *Wait a minute! Why should I worry about what* might *happen? Whatever comes, God will give me the strength to deal with it. Until then, I'm going to move ahead and step out on faith.* I still had trepidation about living out in the wild without running water and electricity (snake country to be sure), but I decided whatever happened, with God's help, I'd deal with it.

■ ■ ■ ■

As soon as school was out, I traveled by myself to California for orientation. From there, I flew to Indonesia, again by myself. On the way, the true irony struck: I was a business major! Why in the world was I going to the jungle?

As the only young woman working on that particular assignment, I spent the entire summer helping a group of missionaries on Kalimantan, a small, remote island in the Indonesian chain with numerous distinct native tribes. I

79

lived with four separate missionary families during my stay, following them around and doing whatever they asked me to do. I prepared meals for visitors, weeded the gardens, dispensed medicine to mothers, and played games with and told Bible stories to children. I spoke to the various tribes in English, telling them of my faith in God, and the missionaries translated my words. I was never sure if I was saying the right things, but I hoped the people would see and feel my love for them.

The result of the trip? It made me more dependent on God's ability to sustain me whether or not I was sure of my own abilities. Merely fulfilling my commitment with a smile was a confidence booster. But by the end of summer, I had also conquered my fear of snakes (almost!) and even felt that I had a small ability to help another human being.

Beyond that, by nature I'm a planner. At that point I already had my future all planned out, and I spent a lot of time thinking through my options, figuring out what I thought was the wisest way to proceed. I sometimes worried about things that were still two years down the road! Going to Indonesia helped me learn how to trust God for my day-to-day existence. I was far out of my personal comfort zone, the zone where I could control things with my own skills, intelligence, and effort—the zone where I felt secure. In Indonesia I was forced to admit, "God, I don't know what I'm doing here, so you have to step up to the plate and help me!" In every situation I encountered, God taught me that I could rely on him for my present as well as my future. No matter what came my way, he was there to help me.

Interestingly, the trip also confirmed my suspicions that I didn't have to go to a foreign country or even be a missionary to be who God wanted me to be. All I had to do was trust him and do my best to follow his plan for my life. Mostly that meant just asking for help and his perspective on all the little everyday situations in life. If I maintained a continual relationship with him, the big picture would take care of itself.

■　■　■　■

While I was at Wheaton, the malpractice suit surrounding my dad's death finally went to trial after seven years. I wasn't sure I could emotionally handle listening to all the details of Dad's death again, especially the "what ifs" and the "could have, should have" aspects of the doctors' and hospital's failure to treat my dad in the best manner.

I was tired of dealing with all that hurt and anger in my life and feeling that I'd been robbed of all the good things I'd anticipated growing up. As much as I tried to keep the bitterness and resentment hemmed in, they seeped out of me ever so slowly . . . almost imperceptibly, like nuclear waste that creeps underground and contaminates everything above the surface. Every once in a while, as I saw the long hours of work and the many sacrifices my mom made to keep life functioning normally for our family after Dad's death, a geyser of bitterness would gush out of me. Selfishly, my anger stemmed not only from Mom's trials but also from seeing friends with their intact families and feeling resentful that I didn't have the same thing. For the most part, I was able to cap my anger quickly, but I knew it was still there, boiling just below the surface of my life.

I had always struggled with the "why" questions in regard to Dad's death. Eventually such questions led me down the road of "It's not fair!" and became a swirling cauldron of anger, bitterness, and resentment deep inside me. I recognized the ugliness of those emotions and didn't want them in my life, but I didn't know what to do about it.

One day I was talking with Dennis Massaro, the director of Wheaton's Office of Christian Outreach, the organization that had arranged our summer mission trip to Indonesia. Somehow the subject turned to the upcoming trial, and I felt the cauldron seething within me. I dumped the whole mess on Dennis, who listened patiently without a word of condemnation.

When I was finally out of words, Dennis calmly said, "You know, Lisa, God knew the hospital they took your dad to wasn't going to have the right equipment to perform the surgery."

I gulped hard, as though I was going to interrupt Dennis, but he paid no attention and kept right on talking. "The Lord knew the first doctor they talked to was going to blow off the situation. At any time, God could have changed the circumstances. He could have changed the hospital or the doctor. Better yet, he could have healed the hole in your dad's heart. But for whatever reason, he let the natural course of things take place that day."

I blinked back tears as Dennis continued. "Knowing

what the consequences were going to be for your family and for you, he nonetheless allowed it to happen. Maybe it's time for you to accept that."

Dennis's gentle words were a targeted arrow in my heart. I knew he was right. And at the same time I both loved and hated him for telling me the truth. But the truth set me free.

My conversation with Dennis reminded me of what I'd read from the Bible just a few nights earlier. So I flipped back to the same passage again. Although I'd read it many times previously, suddenly the words popped off the page at me:

> *Oh, the depth of the riches of the wisdom and knowledge*
> *of God!*
> *How unsearchable his judgments,*
> *and his paths beyond tracing out!*
> *"Who has known the mind of the Lord?*
> *Or who has been his counselor?"*
> *"Who has ever given to God,*
> *that God should repay him?"*
> *For from him and through him and to him are all things.*
> *To him be the glory forever! Amen.*
>
> —Romans 11:33-36

As I read those words, a thought struck me. *Who are you to question God and say that you have a better plan than he does? You don't have the same wisdom and knowledge that he has, or the understanding of the big picture. You think you deserve a happy life and get angry when it doesn't always happen like that.*

In fact, you are a sinner and deserve only death. The fact that God has offered you hope for eternal life is amazing! You should be overwhelmed with joy and gratitude.

All at once I was caught in a dichotomy: I know I'm really important to God and he truly loves me. Yet at the same time, I'm a mere mortal with limited understanding. *Who am I to question him?* I asked myself, realizing, perhaps for the first time, how awe-inspiring God really is. It was then I made a *conscious* decision to stop questioning God and start trusting him.

That brief conversation with Dennis Massaro would become one of the most significant in my life, replaying in my mind over and over in the years—and the tragedy— to come.

8

SURPRISED BY LOVE

ABOUT 12 MONTHS before I graduated from Wheaton College, I began dating a guy I'd met on campus. He had some great character traits, and we developed a strong relationship. For the first time I could imagine wanting to spend the rest of my life with someone. A few months into the relationship, we became engaged.

Yet something inside just wasn't right. Deep down I knew that for all his admirable qualities, this man and I were not right for each other. Besides, I didn't want to marry at 22 or 23. I wanted to succeed on my own first and prove that I could take care of myself. Moreover, I realized that both of us needed more time to mature emotionally. Mom could see it, too, but she didn't want to say anything. Finally, during the summer following graduation in May 1991, she approached me. "I'm only going to say this once, and after I say it, you do whatever you want," she began. Then she openly expressed her concerns about my relationship with my fiancé.

That same week, my good friend and lifelong mentor, Joe Urbanowicz, called and asked me to have lunch with him. Joe and I talked about my graduation and future plans. Then, with no knowledge of what Mom and I had discussed, Joe expressed almost the identical concerns Mom had mentioned.

I knew I had to call off the wedding.

I had already graduated and had a job lined up with an accounting firm in the Chicago area starting in September, so I returned to Glen Ellyn, near Wheaton, to work. Originally I planned simply to postpone the wedding, but when I got back to Wheaton and discussed the situation with my fiancé, we decided to break up completely.

For a while I was quite content by myself. I had just come out of a serious relationship, so I wasn't looking for another one. I was only 22 years old. I had a cute little apartment over a shop in Glen Ellyn, with my own furniture and decorations, my own car, and a new job. What else in life did I need? I got busy putting the finishing touches on my new apartment just as my mom was planning to come to Chicago in November to visit Paul and Holly, who now attended Wheaton College, for Parents' Weekend. Because of her work schedule, Mom hadn't been able to attend many campus events, and I wanted everything to be just right for her.

Little did I know that in September of that same year, Todd and some buddies of his were discussing me and my future. While Todd and longtime friend Keith Franz were staying at Keith's parents' home in Medinah, another friend—Dave Ochs—stopped by. According to Keith, Dave told Todd, "I have some great news for you."

"Oh, really? What's that?"

"Lisa Brosious broke off her engagement."

Todd's eyes opened wide, as though he'd just seen or heard something amazing. "Are you serious?" he asked.

"Sure enough."

Shortly after that, another friend, Steve Hellier, and Todd saw me at church, sitting with some friends. "You ought to ask her out," Steve suggested to Todd as he nodded toward me.

"Naaah, she's still hooked on that other guy."

"No, she's not," Steve insisted.

"Well, I don't have her phone number."

"If I get her number, will you ask her out?"

"All right; that's a deal. You get her number, and I'll ask her out."

Unknown to me at the time, Steve called one of my friends and found out my phone number.

A few weeks later, in late October, Todd called my apartment, but I wasn't home. Kara, my former college roommate, was visiting and took the message.

When I got back, Kara told me, "Todd Beamer called."

"What?" I remembered Todd from the Senior Seminar class, but I hadn't talked with him in six months. And even then I hadn't *really* talked with him much.

"Yeah, I think he wanted to ask you out," Kara said with a smile.

"What are you talking about? I'm sure he just wanted to talk about work, or maybe he needs somebody's phone number or something."

"Maybe," Kara said with a shrug, "but I really think he wants to ask you for a date."

Curious, I called Todd back that night, and we exchanged small talk for nearly half an hour. We were having such a good time that I was a little off guard when Todd said, "I was just calling to see what you're doing for Saturday night and was wondering if you'd like to go out and get some dinner or something."

My heart fluttered a bit as I considered the invitation, but then I remembered—*Mom's coming!*

"Well, I don't know," I replied slowly. "My mom's coming in for Parents' Weekend. Let me call you back."

Todd may have thought I was hedging, but I wasn't. Mom really *was* coming to visit. I called her to see if she minded me going out during her stay. "Oh, no, Lisa. Go!" she encouraged me.

I called Todd back and accepted his invitation.

When Mom arrived that weekend, I brought her to my apartment and helped her get settled in. Mom later told me she had a strange intuition about my first date with Todd. "I didn't want to scare him," she said, "but I just had a feeling I needed to meet this guy." The night of Todd's and my date, however, Mom went out to dinner with Holly and Paul before Todd arrived.

Todd came to the apartment to pick me up for our first date on November 2, 1991. The evening started off poorly. Under normal conditions, Chicago is known as the Windy City, and the weather was unusually wet and windy that night. Walking down the streets, Todd and I literally had to lean into the wind to keep from falling over. Todd wasn't sure where the restaurant was located, so we walked for a long time!

We went to a pizza place in town called the Chicago Pizza and Oven Grinder Co. The restaurant was packed with people, and we had to wait for two hours just to get a table. The waiters and waitresses scurried from table to table, but the service was extremely slow. Under ordinary circumstances that could have been a disaster—"First date plus long wait equals awkward conversation." But not for Todd and me. The delay was actually a blessing. We talked nonstop for several hours. We really didn't know each other well, so we discussed all sorts of things—everything from school to our family backgrounds to the arts. "What kind of music do you like?" Todd asked.

"Well, I like all kinds, but I really like country music," I replied.

"No, you don't!" Todd replied, wide-eyed.

"Yes, I do." I couldn't believe I was admitting such a thing, but it was true, so why not? I had actually acquired a taste for country music through a friend of mine.

Just then a country song came on the restaurant speaker system. "Okay, what's that song?" Todd asked, playfully testing me.

" 'All My Ex's Live in Texas,' " I answered, "by George Strait."

"Wow!" Todd exclaimed. "You really do listen to country music!"

Our bill came to a grand total of $21 that night, but we should have paid much more. We occupied a table for several hours!

From our first date, it was clear to me that Todd was a guy who had a clear focus on life. I admired that he had a strong work ethic *and* a direction in life in which he wanted to go. He told me he wanted to finish his master's degree in business. *Mmm,* I thought. *Motivated, intelligent, fun to be with, great sense of humor, quick to smile, and funny, too. This guy could be a keeper.*

For our second date, we went to the circus in Chicago, and when Todd took me home, he kissed me for the first time. I was definitely interested in having another date!

One day, after we'd been dating for a few months, we realized we needed to clarify where we were in our relationship. We knew we had something special, but neither of us wanted to push ahead too rapidly. We beat around the bush for a while concerning just what sort of expectations we both had. Finally Todd ventured, "Well, would it be so bad to be my girlfriend?"

"No," I said with a smile as I hugged him. "I think I'd like that."

Todd was only the second guy I'd ever dated for more than a month or so. I wasn't seeking perfection, but I definitely wanted someone with whom I could have mutual respect, someone strong enough to be comfortable with my strengths. I wanted someone who had enough self-esteem that I wouldn't roll over him with my personality, but not so strong that we were going to clash all the time.

Todd was perfect for me because he was willing to stand up for what he felt passionately about, yet he was not a controlling sort of person. He was gracious and humble but had a healthy self-esteem. He respected my opinions, but if he didn't agree with me, he wasn't afraid to say so. On the other hand, he didn't expect me to be a fawning, brainless automaton, unwilling to challenge him.

I knew Todd cared for his family, too. He spoke often with his sisters and parents, and I saw that as a good thing. I thought, *Most likely, he will one day love his own wife and children in a similar way.*

The only time we ever came close to breaking up was after we'd been dating about a year. Todd was working on his M.B.A. at DePaul University in Chicago, and I hardly ever saw him! He was gone every night, with classes four nights a week. In between he studied all the time, prepared papers, and worked a regular job. I was glad he was so focused on acquiring his degree, and I didn't want to discourage him in any way, but I could see the handwriting on the wall. This was the way things were going to be. While we were both highly motivated and goal oriented, our ideas of success and what it might take to get there were on parallel but not intersecting paths.

Todd was a hard worker, and that was a plus, but he tended toward being a workaholic. That was unacceptable to me, and it created tension in our relationship. Even before we married, we considered the difficult issue that my expectations were not being met by reality. Either I could adjust my expectations, or reality needed to change.

One night we were sitting in his car outside his apartment, talking about the fact that we hadn't seen each other a lot lately. I didn't give him an ultimatum—choose one or the other, either the M.B.A. or me—but I emphatically said,

"Todd, I want you to know that I am not happy with what's going on right now."

Todd was equally forthright. "Part of it is nonnegotiable; this is what I have to do right now. I really want to get this degree done. I don't want to drag it out. At the same time I don't want to lose you for the sake of an M.B.A. What can we do to make both things happen?"

We were stuck at an impasse, neither of us willing to back off from what we needed. We compromised by agreeing to disagree, but conflict over Todd's working too much—along with the anger it elicited in me and how I confronted it—was the one area that would rear its head again and again in our relationship. At least we were aware of the potential potholes before we started down the path of "marital bliss." We knew exactly where the tension would lie . . . and we weren't wrong.

■　■　■　■

While Todd was busy working on his M.B.A., I spent much of my spare time mentoring high school students at College Church in Wheaton. Knowing the impact that my youth leaders, Joe and Karen Urbanowicz, had upon me during my teenage years, I'd always had a heart for youth work. While in college I had worked in Chicago's inner city, tutoring young girls. After college I worked mostly at College Church, where I mentored a small group of teenage girls for about three years. Todd stopped by occasionally to say hello to the girls in our group, and it was obvious they were impressed with him. I looked forward to the day when he and I might work together, helping young people.

Not yet, though. For now Todd had to stay focused on working his way through graduate school. At the time of his graduation from Wheaton, Todd had a job with his mentor and former sixth-grade teacher, Steve Johnson. Steve still lived in Wheaton, where he owned a small computer company. Steve and Todd were perfect partners: Steve made the computers, and Todd loved to sell them.

Todd worked with Steve for several months following graduation before going to work for Wilson Sporting Goods in 1992. For Todd, working in a sports environment was like being paid to visit heaven. Occasionally superstar athletes visited Wilson's home office, adding extra excitement during the workday. On more than a few occasions, Todd called me from work, nearly bursting with excitement. "Lisa, guess who is in the building!"

"I have no idea. . . ."

"Frank Thomas is here today!" The consummate fan, Todd sometimes asked the receptionist if he could have the day's sign-in sheet. There on the sheet would be the superstar's autograph, and like a satisfied little boy at the ballpark, Todd would tuck the sheet away for safekeeping.

The ultimate came one day when Michael Jordan stopped by. Todd called me and in an excited whisper said, "I know he's here in the building somewhere. I'm going to go out and walk the halls to see if I can find him!" I'm not sure how long it took him that day, but Todd "accidentally" passed Michael Jordan in the hall. He didn't really get to meet Michael, but just to think that he might have touched the same door that Michael touched thrilled Todd.

He worked for Wilson about a year and a half before he finally took a break for about six months to work full-time on his M.B.A. It was a time to celebrate when Todd received his M.B.A. from DePaul University during the summer of 1993.

■ ■ ■ ■

Once we started dating, we never dated anyone else, but we still proceeded in our relationship slowly. We didn't say "I love you" to each other until the anniversary of our first date. We didn't talk about marriage for several months after that. We'd dated for more than two full years by the time we got engaged.

As we thought about marriage and our future plans, we decided to consider moving to the East Coast. Todd, with M.B.A. in hand, was looking for a new job anyway, and both our families were in the East now. (Todd's family had moved to the Washington, D.C., area.) In the fall of 1993 Todd began interviewing for various positions from Boston to Washington, D.C. He used my mom's house in New York as home base while I stayed at my job in Chicago. Just before Thanksgiving I came home, and Todd was already there with my family.

Keeping with our Thanksgiving tradition of hiking up Turkey Mountain, Todd and I made the trek up the slope on November 24, Todd's birthday. It was a crisp, cool day, and when we reached the peak, we looked out over the incredible view. The New York City skyline was visible in the distance, and we could clearly make out the Empire

State Building and the World Trade Center towers. We were talking about our future when Todd suddenly asked, "Well, would it be so bad to be my wife?" hearkening back to the question he'd asked me when we first started dating. The twinkle in Todd's eyes told me he was asking me to marry him.

"No," I said, "but if this is a proposal, shouldn't I say yes?"

"Well, will you marry me then?"

"Yes, Todd, I will marry you!"

He pulled out an engagement ring and placed it on my finger.

Todd later teased me as to why he wanted to get engaged on his birthday rather than on Thanksgiving or Christmas. "If we get engaged on a holiday, the ring is considered a gift. So if something happens and we break up, I can't get it back!"

There was no danger of him getting the ring back. I was head over heels in love with Todd Beamer.

9

FORWARD THINKING

THE NEXT FEW MONTHS were a mad dash as Todd and I prepared for our wedding on May 14, 1994. I had always wanted to move back East, so I was glad Todd was looking for a job there.

I continued working in Chicago until March. Todd moved to New Jersey in January, when he accepted a new job with the Oracle Corporation, the world's second-largest computer software company. Todd had interviewed with Paul Nix in Oracle's New Jersey office and had hit it off well with him. The job Paul offered held great opportunity for Todd to learn, grow, and move up rapidly within the company. That fit well into Todd's plans, but before accepting the job offer, Todd asked for a week off in May for a honeymoon!

Our wedding took place at the First Baptist Church in Peekskill, New York, the church I had attended most of my life. Keith Franz was Todd's best man, and my sister, Holly, was my maid of honor.

Unknown to me at the time, Keith carried a disposable camera with him onto the platform. He covertly planned to take a picture of Todd's and my first married kiss—during the ceremony. The night before, at the wedding rehearsal, Keith had given Todd specific instructions on how he should kiss me. "In order for this to work, when you kiss Lisa, you have to lean left. If you lean right, all I'll get will be a picture of the back of your head."

"Dude, I don't ever lean left," Todd said.

Before and even during the wedding ceremony, Keith reminded Todd again and again. "Lean left!" he whispered.

When the big moment arrived, Todd started to kiss me as usual, then hesitated a second and moved his face to the left. Suddenly Keith jumped out of place, and a flash went off in our eyes, capturing my look of surprise as Keith jubilantly took the picture. The entire congregation broke up in laughter. It was typical of Keith and Todd that even in our wedding—*especially* in our wedding—they were having fun.

Our reception was at the Cortlandt Yacht Club overlooking the Hudson River. On our way in to the reception, Keith and his buddies engineered a sneak attack with Silly String. He and the other groomsmen sprayed us with gobs of the stuff! I was smiling and waving as we made our way through the crowd, but in my mind I was saying, *I hope this stuff comes off my dress, or you're gonna get it, Keith!*

Fortunately the string peeled off, though not without some time and effort on Todd's and my part.

When we finally got in the car and headed toward the airport, Todd and I looked at each other impishly, and I said, "We did it! We're married!"

■　■　■　■

We honeymooned for a week at Seabrook Island, near Charleston, South Carolina, and then it was back to New Jersey to begin "real life."

After settling in, I got a job with Oracle selling educational services, and for a while, Todd and I worked in the same sales office near Newark. We enjoyed being able to discuss work situations over dinner, and even after I quit working outside the home, my experience with Oracle helped me understand the stress and pressures on Todd in such a competitive corporate environment. Not everyone enjoys that sort of competition, but Todd thrived on it.

We set up housekeeping in a small apartment in Plainsboro, New Jersey, a short drive from Princeton. I brought some furniture—a table, some chairs, a love seat, and a few other items—from my apartment in Glen Ellyn; Todd brought his huge Michael Jordan poster and hung it in our kitchen!

We began our life together with all the hopes, dreams, and aspirations typical of most college-educated couples in the mid-1990s. As two goal-oriented, type A people, Todd and I planned every little detail of our lives, including our career courses and our personal lives. We left very little to chance or to accident. For instance, we planned to get Todd's career off the ground, buy a house, and have adequate insurance coverage before having children. Like most young couples just starting out in life, we naively thought we could control our own destiny.

We had clear ideas about what our life should look like.

In fact, back in 1992, as Todd was beginning his work toward his M.B.A., he had made a list of values and characteristics he wanted to identify in his life. Always a forward thinker, he also developed a list of goals that he wanted to accomplish by the time he was 30.

The qualities Todd wrote down on his list were almost prophetic:

- Be self-sufficient and a good provider.
- Be a leader in society.
- Have a comfortable home, nice cars, and a "mahogany room."

Todd wanted a distinguished, dark den or a library-style office—the Beamer room, as he referred to it—where he could retreat from the world and recharge his batteries. When we finally built a home office for him, it was actually bright, cheery, and surrounded with windows—not stuffy looking at all.

- Be a strong Christian, know direction, and be disciplined.
- Be a father with integrity.
- Be able to build friendships, take care of and assist friends.
- Love my wife and support her efforts.
- Maybe develop a hobby such as photography, maybe write a book.
- Strive to be like my father—to be respected even when I'm not around.
- I want to fly below the radar screen.

Todd often talked about "flying below the radar screen." By this he meant he wanted to be inconspicuous and to maintain a low profile. This was partly because he was humble and partly because he enjoyed holding his cards close to his vest. He didn't want to let the competition know what he was capable of doing or what he planned to do until he was ready to rise to the fore. That's how he operated in his business dealings—always friendly, competent, and prepared, but allowing other people to sing his praises rather than flaunting his successes or tooting his own horn.

- Have a meaningful job and career.
- Know important people—I will be important.
- Continue education.
- Travel to Europe several times.
- Have good values.
- Good health.
- 100 percent committed to relationships.
- Wealth and security.
- Control my destiny and environment so I can have free time to spend with my family.
- Be compassionate to others—support through time and money.
- Own my own business.

Todd always had a desire to do something beyond just working at a job. He envisioned himself as a coach, encouraging others to do their best. He sometimes talked about going into a coaching career after he had accomplished his goals in the business world. Some of his desires penned on September 9, 1992, are especially poignant as I read them today:

- Live to an old age.
- Contentment in life and to be satisfied.
- Arrive at the road's end with satisfaction, and don't look back.

In July of 1993, after Todd had completed his M.B.A., he wrote out a similar list of his goals. In it, he prioritized what he believed would lead him to accomplish success and contentment. At the top of the list was his spiritual life, followed by his relationships, his career, and his desire for continued education. That was the order Todd strove to maintain as he sifted through life's many choices and the voices vying for his attention.

■ ■ ■ ■

Todd was especially wise when it came to saving and handling money. Like most other areas of his life, he had clear ideas of how he hoped to earn, save, and invest. In defining his goals in 1992—before he'd even had a full-time job—he wrote out how he planned to be financially secure by the time he was 30 years of age! He figured it all out, how he needed to save and then invest his money at a good interest rate while continuing to add to his net worth each year. Todd refused to spend money on frivolous, discretionary items until he had fulfilled his savings obligations.

My attitudes toward money were similar to Todd's, so money never became a divisive issue in our marriage. While we enjoyed buying and having nice things, we both believed in saving money, living frugally, and operating debt-free as much as possible. After living in our apartment for a year, we bought our first house, a nice but older home in nearby Hightstown, New Jersey, where we lived for five years. According to our plan, we were right on track.

In 1994 Keith, Todd's longtime buddy, came to visit, and we drove in to New York City to show him the sights. We did all the tourist things, including riding the elevator to the top of the Empire State Building to view the skyline. "Whew! That's really a long way down!" said Todd as he and Keith peered out over the edge and down to the ground. Keith took a picture of Todd and me with the skyline as the backdrop. We looked like a couple of typical tourists, with Todd wearing one of his many baseball hats, the wind whipping at our faces, and the two enormous towers of the World Trade Center in the background.

Not long after that, Keith informed us that he was planning to get married. Obviously he was excited about getting engaged, but Todd wasn't so sure. Todd loved his friend, and he wasn't afraid to confront him and say hard things when he needed to. He was concerned that Keith and his fiancée, Sandy Kujawski, might be moving too quickly. After meeting on a blind date in June 1994 and dating for a very short time, they were talking about getting married in August 1995! For meticulous planners like Todd and me, that was extremely fast.

Todd wrote Keith a kind, gracious letter, but he pulled

no punches. "Are you sure you know what you're doing?" Todd wrote to him. "It seems as though you are moving kind of quickly. If God is in this marriage, I don't want to slow it down. But at the same time, if you're not sure, don't push it."

Keith appreciated Todd's willingness to confront him and recognized the fact that his friend really cared for him. He assured Todd that he and Sandy were right for each other and ready to be married. "In fact, I'd be honored if you would be my best man." Keith and Sandy got married on August 26, 1995, and Todd was Keith's best man. To nobody's surprise, Todd took a picture of Keith and Sandy during their first married kiss, and yes, he made sure the couple was tangled in Silly String before leaving the reception!

■ ■ ■ ■

True to Paul Nix's predictions, Todd advanced rapidly on the Oracle career track. He poured himself into his job, doing whatever needed to be done. No task was insignificant, no job too menial. If Todd could do it, he was there. Todd started with Oracle in 1994 as a field marketing representative, developing software marketing seminars and materials for the New Jersey sales force. He was only 25 years old, extremely young for that position, but Oracle believed in Todd, and Todd had tremendous confidence that he could do the job. By 1995 Todd was promoted to associate account manager—his first real sales position for Oracle. He assisted Frank McMahon, a senior account manager, and within another year had worked himself into an account manager position with his own account list. The job required more travel, but it seemed a small price to pay for the potential success within Todd's grasp.

Todd was an extremely good salesperson. He was people-focused and an exceptionally good listener. Anyone who talked with Todd felt he was giving them his undivided attention.

■　■　■　■

One of the keys to getting acclimated to our new area was becoming involved in a local church. When we first moved to New Jersey, Todd and I visited several congregations, searching for a "spiritual home." We were pleasantly surprised when we discovered a large group of people our age at Princeton Alliance Church, an eclectic congregation linked to the Christian and Missionary Alliance denomination. Todd and I didn't know much about the church's history, but the congregation was friendly, the teachings of the Bible were made relevant to our lives, and we felt an immediate affinity. We became involved in the activities of the church and formed many solid friendships—relationships that would prove invaluable in the years ahead.

One group that Todd and I became a part of was a Care Circle, several young couples who usually met once a week on Sunday evening to talk about life issues in relation to our faith. Sometimes our discussion centered around a book we had all agreed to read; often the conversation focused on husband-and-wife relationships or other topics relating to spiritual growth. The group was more than merely a gab session. We frequently prayed with and for each other, as various members experienced tremendous victories and horrible defeats, great achievements and traumatic events in their lives. When Todd and I first joined the care group, most of the members were married, without children. Before long, our group boasted more than 15 kids among us, and parenting issues were added to our conversations.

After we'd lived in New Jersey for a few years, most of our closest friendships revolved around our church and our care group. Todd and several of the guys—including Brian Mumau, Doug MacMillan, George Pittas, Steve Mayer, Axel Johnson, and John Edgar Caterson—started meeting for breakfast at 6:30 A.M. on Friday mornings in an accountability group. The group's primary purpose was to help the guys maintain a healthy balance between spiritual priorities and home/career responsibilities. They did everything together: played on the church softball team, did home improvement projects, and at least once a year went on a special guys-only weekend golf trip.

We had no idea how special those relationships would become to all of us.

Even before Todd and I had children of our own, the church's youth pastor, Scott McKee, pulled us into working with the high-school-aged kids in the church. At first we started "team teaching" the teens' Sunday school class— one of us would teach while the other maintained order. We enjoyed being with the kids so much, before long we were involved with the Wednesday-night youth program as well.

As the youth group grew, we soon ran out of classroom space in our church building, so we met in an old tractor trailer that had been put up on blocks behind the church. We nicknamed the trailer "The Growth Coach," and some of the kids called it "The Roach Coach." For the most part, though, they loved it!

Some of the kids in the class had the same sort of questions I had battled as a teenager after my dad's death, so I was able to identify with them and help them work through their answers.

Todd always went straight for the tough guys—the ones who looked as though they weren't interested and that nothing spiritual mattered to them. Todd often used sports to relate to the guys, first winning them over as friends, then sharing his faith with them.

Similar to most church youth groups, we taught the Bible, but we also talked about all the hot-button issues the kids were dealing with on a daily basis—drugs, sex, eating disorders, self-esteem issues, destructive behavior patterns, suicide, and others. Rather than simply saying "Do this" or "Don't do that," we attempted to present truth positively and let the kids understand why certain things were wrong and how other things could enhance their relationships with God, friends, parents, and siblings.

Todd especially wanted to make sure that we dealt with character issues. He wanted our young friends to develop biblically based, solid character, so no matter what situation they found themselves in, they could make the right decision. "Decisions you make in high school will affect you the rest of your life," he often told the kids.

Todd was always a "forward thinker," good with setting goals and then avoiding anything that might hinder his progress. He was hard on himself, too. I used to tease him, "Todd, lighten up. You're going to have three or four midlife crises before the age of 30!" But Todd always had a plan. He was going somewhere, and he carried that same enthusiasm to his work with the kids. It genuinely bothered him when he saw one of them doing something self-destructive or making unwise decisions. He'd throw an arm around a teenage guy and say something like, "Dude, can't you see that what you're doing could possibly mess up the rest of your life?"

Often the young people would begin to make changes in their lives simply because they knew Todd really cared about them. He wasn't trying to lay a big spiritual line on them. He was concerned about them. He often called the members of the youth group who seemed to need more personal attention. "Just wanted to see how you're doing today." Todd spent so much time on the phone for his job, it seemed that the last thing he'd want to do would be to dial up someone's number that he didn't really have to call. But he cared about those teenagers so much that he never considered it an inconvenience either to call them or talk to them when they phoned us. If we missed their calls but got a message, he was quick to return their calls.

Todd often drove the church van for youth-group trips, camps, and weekend retreats. Both of us loved country music—especially artists such as Alan Jackson, Clint Black, Garth Brooks, Wynonna Judd, and Dwight Yoakam—and the kids hated it. When Todd put his favorite country CDs in and cranked them up, the New Jersey kids would go wild! "Turn that stuff off!"

Todd just smiled and turned his country music up louder. He loved to sing along and he did . . . loudly . . . though completely off-key. Everyone would dissolve into laughter and yelling until Todd finally acquiesced and allowed the kids to put some of their favorite music in the CD player. It was funny to watch him try to understand the rap lyrics to make sure they weren't objectionable. The kids didn't mind his scrutiny since they loved him, and it was obvious he loved them. Better yet, he had a good influence on them.

I couldn't wait to see the influence he'd have when we had children of our own.

10

ADDING TO
OUR TEAM

WHILE TODD AND I were still dating, we discussed our desire to have children someday. Todd came from a family of three siblings, and I came from a family of four, so we decided three children would be perfect for us.

Once we were married, we planned for our pregnancies as much as possible, but we were still delightfully surprised when we learned in spring 1997 that our first child was due on Christmas Day. After finding out I was pregnant, we went to a picnic that afternoon at the home of our friends Doug and Chivon MacMillan. Although we didn't tell any of our friends the news about my pregnancy, every time we heard a gleeful outburst from one of the children frolicking in the grass, Todd and I would gaze at each other knowingly, as if to say, *What are we doing? We are going to be parents! We've started down this road and there's no turning back!*

We were excited and ready for kids—well, as ready as any couple ever is to have their whole life turned upside down. We'd been married for three years. We were settled in the community, had purchased a home, and had built up some savings. We'd also traveled extensively to places such as Yellowstone National Park, Hawaii, Mexico, Bermuda, and to various vacation spots in South Carolina. While I was pregnant with our first child, we went to Europe on vacation. "We won't be able to do these kinds of trips so easily once we have kids," Todd said.

We had anticipated that when we had children, I would stay at home. I didn't see being a stay-at-home mom as a sacrifice of my career; to me, raising our children was the most important career I could ever have! Even before I became pregnant, Todd and I lived on his income alone. We worked our monthly budget off his income, using my paycheck for special purchases and savings. That way when it came time for me to stay home with our children, it wouldn't be a radical change in our lifestyle and pinch us financially. My manager at Oracle also allowed me to work part-time at home, which I did for about two years after our first baby was born. I was grateful for the opportunity to work, but to Todd and me, our family was our first priority.

■ ■ ■ ■

Christmas Day 1997 came and went, and I was still pregnant. January 5 arrived and still no baby. We went to see our doctor, and she said, "We'll need to induce labor tomorrow morning. Meet me at the hospital at 7:00 A.M."

That night after dinner, I started packing up a few things to take with me to the hospital. Then, around 10:30,

I began to feel extremely uncomfortable. I went upstairs and told Todd, "I don't know what this is, but I don't feel right."

"Are you having contractions?"

"I don't know. . . . I feel these horrible waves of pain in my stomach."

Todd was sure I was in labor. "Okay, let's check to see how far apart these contractions are." Todd pulled out a watch and started timing. He grabbed some paper and wrote down each time I doubled over in pain. A few minutes later, he said, "I think this is for real. The contractions are coming every two minutes!"

"What? That's impossible! You're an idiot!" I blurted through my pain. "It can't happen that fast."

"No, they are!" Todd exclaimed calmly but emphatically.

Before I knew it, I was in the throes of another contraction and stretched out on the bathroom floor. When I started throwing up, Todd got really nervous. The hospital was at least a 45-minute drive from our home, and no doubt Todd was having visions of delivering our first child single-handedly.

"I'm calling the doctor!" Todd insisted.

"No, don't call the doctor," I said. "It's not time yet! She'll think we're idiots!"

"I'm calling." Todd dialed the doctor's number, and sure enough, she said, "Well, let's just see where this goes. . . ."

"No," Todd stated emphatically. "My wife is on the bathroom floor. She's throwing up, and her contractions are about a minute apart. I really think we need to come in to the hospital."

The doctor agreed, so we piled into the car, and I leaned back, shut my eyes, and prayed we'd get to the hospital in time. Fortunately, at this hour of night, the traffic was light. Todd focused on the road, and I was in no condition to carry on light conversation, so we made the 45-minute trip almost in silence. As Todd whipped the car into the emergency-room parking area, our baby was already about to be born.

The hospital personnel brought out a gurney, lifted me onto it, and raced down the hallway. Todd ran into the birthing room behind me. We'd barely been at the hospital an hour when we heard the cry of a newborn baby. "It's a boy!" the doctor announced.

We hadn't been certain whether we were having a boy or a girl. We really didn't want to know ahead of time; we wanted to be surprised. Todd was elated to have a little boy! Good thing, because we hadn't really settled on any girls' names. But we were absolutely certain what name we wanted for our first son: David Paul—David for Todd's dad and Paul after my father.

Reminiscent of the scene in the Disney animated movie *The Lion King* where Mufasa, the father lion, holds the new baby lion, Simba, high above his head for the world to see, Todd was so excited he hoisted David high in the air, like a champion lifting up a trophy.

"*Ahem*, we're going to take the baby out to be measured," one of the nurses said, reaching up to retrieve David from Todd's grasp.

"I'll go with you," Todd volunteered. He was protective of our children right from the start. He'd heard horror stories of babies being switched at birth, and he didn't want to take any chances. "Are you okay?" He leaned over my bed's side rail. "I really want to stay with them to make sure nobody switches our baby."

"Go," I think I replied, enjoying Todd's excitement.

Todd followed the nurse out of the delivery room and kept a close watch on everything that was going on. By the time I was settled into a hospital room and the nurses brought David in to me, Todd had retrieved our video camera from the car and was playing Cecil B. DeMille. He was videotaping everything! It was about 2:00 A.M. on January 6. We debated about calling our parents in the middle of the night, but we couldn't wait. Despite the hour, they were elated with the news and with David Paul's name.

When I was discharged from the hospital, a nurse brought me down to the front of the hospital in a wheelchair, while Todd went for the car. Todd was so cute! He continued videotaping the entire procedure, driving through the hospital parking lot and giving a play-by-play commentary as though creating a documentary. He videotaped himself driving through the parking garage: "Now we're passing these cars, and we're driving up to the front door, and I think I see Mom and David. . . ." To say that Todd was excited about being a dad would be like saying that Michael Jordan is okay at playing basketball!

My mom was with us when we brought David home from the hospital. Todd took him inside the house, and David immediately started squalling. Todd carried David around the house, showing him his new toys, his room, and all sorts of other things that an infant could care less about.

Finally, in exasperation, Todd looked at David, who was still bawling. "What?" Todd asked. "You're disappointed?" Eventually we realized David needed his diaper changed.

With David screaming, Mom, Todd, and I attempted to change the baby's diaper on the bed. Believe it or not, it took all three of us to clean up the mess. We not only made a mess of David's diaper, we messed up his clothes and the bedspread as well. Poor David! If he could have talked, he might have said something like, "These are not the parents I signed up for!"

The night we came home from the hospital with David, Todd was faced with his first test of fatherhood. Months earlier he had purchased tickets to take a client to the Chicago Bulls versus the New York Knicks basketball game in New York City. Michael Jordan, Todd's favorite athlete, was still playing for the Bulls, and the Bulls-Knicks game was a perennial sellout because of the huge rivalry between the teams. Before buying the tickets, Todd had asked me about how I'd feel about his going out to the game so soon after the birth of our baby, and I'd told him it would be fine. Of course, at the time we were thinking our baby would be born at Christmas. Now the game was on David's first night in his new environment. I knew Todd really wanted to go to the game, but he also wanted to be home with David and me.

"Go ahead and go," I told Todd. "I'll be fine."

Todd reluctantly agreed. When he came home around 1:00 A.M., I was up feeding David and wasn't feeling well. I was exhausted—and must have looked it, too. "How was the game?" I asked when Todd came in. "Did you have a good time?"

"Oh, it was okay," he said tentatively.

"Okay? You better tell me it was better than okay!"

Then Todd smiled broadly. "It was fantastic, and I'm glad I went. I just didn't want you to feel bad."

Todd was the consummate father, doting over David's every move and always trying to teach him something new. Most evenings those first few months, Todd took care of David, lying with him on the couch so they could watch sports on television together. I laughed when I saw them— like father, like son.

"You know, you may think you're being a really great dad right now, but it's going to get a lot tougher than this," I warned Todd whimsically. "In a few months, he's not going to want to just sit on the couch and watch football and basketball games anymore."

"I know," Todd replied, "but I'm hoping that if I start him young, we'll have lots of things in common when he grows up."

■ ■ ■ ■

Two years later our second baby was also overdue, so this time we induced labor. While we waited for the Pitocin to take effect, Todd and the doctor talked about the doctor's hobbies of stamp collecting and photography. Both electronics enthusiasts, they discussed the pros and cons of various brands of electronic equipment such as DVD players. For a while I joined in the conversation; then my labor became more intense. "Ah, guys, could you take that conversation elsewhere?" I finally groused when they continued to "talk shop," sounding like the latest issue of *Consumer Reports*. "I've got a few other things going on here!"

When the baby was born—another boy—I could tell immediately by Todd's facial expression that something was wrong. Always calm under pressure, Todd never lost his composure, but the look in his eyes told me we had a problem. Apparently the umbilical cord had gotten wrapped tightly around the baby, and the doctors had to work quickly to unbind the baby so he could breathe.

When the cord was finally unwound and everyone was breathing easier, including Todd and me, we named our new baby. Todd liked the name Andrew, especially Drew, and I wanted a boy named after Todd, so we named him Andrew Todd Beamer.

As we had done with David two years earlier, we dedicated Drew to God in a ceremony at our church. Todd and I stood in front of the congregation with our children, and Todd said, "Andrew is the name of one of Jesus' first disciples. His example is one we hope our son Drew will follow as he grows." Todd went on to explain that after meeting Jesus, one of the first things Andrew did was to go find his brother Peter and introduce him to Jesus.

"This story gives us a perfect example of what our reaction is to be when we meet Jesus," Todd continued. "Follow him immediately and then bring others."

While Todd was being so serious, the audience was

smiling and chuckling. Our two-year-old son, David, was roaming around the platform as Todd spoke, exploring and having a good time, and the congregation was loving it! Finally, as David made a pass nearby, Todd reached down and scooped him up as though nothing out of the ordinary was going on, never missing a beat of his talk.

David kicked off his shoe, to the audience's delight, but Todd managed to finish on a poignant note. "The name *Andrew* means 'with strength and wisdom,' " Todd said. "We have chosen a verse of dedication for Drew today that will remind him his strength is not from his own physical, mental, or spiritual abilities but only from one source, and that is Jesus. As he strives to be a fully devoted follower of Christ, we pray he will remember the promise of Philippians 4:13: *I can do everything through him who gives me strength.*" It was a promise Todd believed as much for himself as for our boys and me.

■　■　■　■

Having two children resulted in a bit of a surprise. We had anticipated that the workload for two children would simply be double that of one child. Wrong! Suddenly it seemed there were never enough hands to get everything done, or enough hours in the day.

When Drew was born, we were in the midst of searching out and buying property, and preparing to build our "dream home." Between the stress of building a new house, work responsibilities, and caring for the kids, Todd and I both felt maxed out most of the time. Every parent of kids under two knows that exhausted feeling and claims that deeply spiritual promise: This too shall pass. One night, as I was busy preparing dinner, Todd came in from work and found David and Drew both fussing incessantly. "Now I know why so many parents stop after having two kids," Todd joked.

■ ■ ■ ■

From the time the boys were able to stand, Todd was already teaching them how to throw and catch a ball. In fact, when David was only a month or two old, Todd bought him a red Michael Jordan basketball.

"Todd, he's not going to be able to play with this ball," I said.

"I know, I know," he replied. "But someday he will."

Any time Todd traveled to a city with a major sports team, he brought the boys back something sports related. For instance, he traveled to St. Louis the season Mark McGwire broke the home-run record, so Todd brought home a McGwire shirt for Drew and a batting helmet for David.

Todd found it almost impossible to pass by a sports store if he had the boys with him. When David was only three, he became enamored with Major League Baseball catchers. David watched the games on TV with Todd, and he thought the catcher's equipment was really special.

Todd asked me, "What do you think? Should I buy him some catcher's equipment?"

"Todd!" I exclaimed. "I'm going to be the one home all day trying to strap his knee pads on, and his chest protector, and I just won't have time to keep up with him. So don't get it yet."

Not long after that, I went away for the weekend with some friends from our church. When I came home, Todd looked guilty. "We were out at The Sports Authority," he explained, "and we saw the knee pads, and they were the right size. . . ."

"Todd!"

"Well, they had the catcher's mask, too, but I didn't buy anything else. . . ."

"Todd!"

Not long after that, we went to Home Depot to pick up some things for the house. While I was looking for house-wares, Todd took the boys next door to The Sports Authority.

"We're not going to buy anything," Todd promised. "We're just going to go in and play with some of the new balls."

But we came away from The Sports Authority with a catcher's chest protector, so now David has the entire catcher's gear . . . and I'm still the one helping him strap it all on!

Todd always thought of the boys when it came time for the Super Bowl, as well. I nearly cracked up laughing when I came in one January afternoon and saw Todd and David glued to the television screen on Super Bowl Sunday. Both of them were wearing their Chicago Bears football jerseys while they watched the game. And the Bears weren't even playing! It was especially funny to see Todd in a matching jersey. Todd wouldn't think of wearing anything that matched anyone else—he sometimes changed clothes before we went out if he and I had even dressed similarly. But for the boys, he'd happily don a matching shirt.

Todd was such a great father. He was always extremely patient with the children, and he loved to play with them anytime he could. Even when they were dawdling or dallying, Todd always put a positive spin on his encouragement to the kids. He had a special shrill whistle that he used to get the boys' or my attention sometimes. At other times, he'd say, "Come on, guys, let's go. Get your coats and shoes on; it's time to go. *Let's roll!*"

It was a phrase we used a lot around our house.

11

TROUBLE
AT THE TOP

As OUR BOYS GREW, so did Todd's career at Oracle. He
began developing his own list of accounts—at first less-
profitable ones, those the senior reps didn't want. But Todd
didn't mind. He knew he could learn a lot by working on
small deals, and he'd need all that experience later to meet
his goals of closing the big ones. As he worked his way up
the company ladder, Todd pursued higher-profile
accounts—those requiring harder work to secure and
greater expertise to handle but representing richer opportunities, both creatively and financially. Eventually he whit-
tled down his client roster to half a dozen or so extremely
high-profile, high-maintenance clients.

Most of his initial customers were in New Jersey. But as
he became more successful, more and more of his clients
were multinational companies, requiring Todd to travel
extensively to meet and work with them on the grassroots
level. Much of the software he sold was used in the manu-
facturing of products, so Todd not only needed to evaluate

his clients' needs but also to show them how Oracle's products could improve their company's efficiency and productivity.

Along with his professional success came the respect of his peers and the financial success that Todd had worked hard to achieve. In addition, Oracle offered many incentive programs and rewards for superior sales, and as a top performer, Todd earned numerous award trips. We traveled together with Oracle to wonderful vacation spots such as Maui, Bermuda, Mexico, Venice, and other exotic locations.

Todd traveled so much for business that it was always a treat for us when we could travel for pleasure. We looked forward to the Oracle trips every year.

For our fifth anniversary, I planned a surprise trip for Todd, taking him to Chicago for the weekend and to a Cubs game at Wrigley Field. Todd still regarded Chicago as his hometown, so to return there for our fifth anniversary was a treat. Todd thought he was in heaven!

Todd and I had a lot of other dreams we were excited about seeing fulfilled. For instance, we planned to go on a cruise to Alaska for our 10th wedding anniversary in 2004.

We usually left the boys with my mom when we traveled. However, when David was only 18 months old, we took him to England with us. But David didn't have a great appreciation for the bland British food. Nor did Todd, come to think of it. When Todd spied a McDonald's in Oxford, England, he crowed, "God bless America!"

The only drawback to Todd's success in his career was that it took him away from David, Drew, and me so much of the time. When he wasn't traveling, he was tempted to spend too much time in his home office in the evenings and on weekends. And he even took his computer, cell phone, and Palm Pilot along with him on vacations! I sometimes teased him about his electronic "security blankets." Todd couldn't go anywhere without staying connected to his clients.

Todd and I didn't argue a lot. He was such an easygoing guy, it was almost hard to pick a fight with him. But any conflict and tension we experienced in our marriage usually related to our efforts to balance Todd's work and home responsibilities. How much time and effort should he put into his job? How could he juggle other areas of life and give proper attention to the relationships that were most important to him—namely his relationships with God, his family, and his friends? It was not an issue Todd was unaware of, and he really wanted to fix it. We talked about it often— sometimes heatedly—prayed about it, and talked with friends about it. Todd sought wisdom from his Friday-morning breakfast group as well. George Pittas, one of Todd's golf buddies and a member of the breakfast group, kept a journal of the group members' prayer requests.

"Many of Todd's requests were about his family," George recalls. "He often asked for wisdom in understanding Lisa's needs, for patience, and to cherish the moments with David and Drew."

Todd's greatest desire in life was to be a godly husband and father. Yet he was so driven to succeed in his career, he often found the two goals competing against each other. Todd and Brian Mumau, one of his best friends, had similar struggles. They often strategized and prayed together about their career and home responsibilities. They held each other accountable for following through on commitments with their families. Often a brief cell-phone call or e-mail would remind one or the other to keep his priorities straight.

Early in our relationship, long before we ever started talking about marriage, Todd and I recognized that this balance was going to be difficult for him to maintain. One night as we sat on the steps outside my apartment, Todd was explaining to me why his family had moved to California from Wheaton, and some of the sacrifices his dad had made for his job over the years. "A lot of my family's moves were necessary because of my dad's job opportunities," Todd concluded.

I sat quietly for a few moments and then said, "Just so you know . . . I don't know where this relationship is going, but if you and I end up together, we're not going to have that level of commitment to a job. I don't want to move my family around for the sake of a job unless it's absolutely necessary."

"That's legitimate," Todd replied. "I really want to keep it all in balance."

I respected Todd's work ethic immensely and recognized it as being integral to his success, but I could also see red flags raised occasionally by the compulsive side of his personality. Todd's professional goals and expectations for himself were his greatest allies but also could be his greatest enemies. He could sometimes be unrealistic in thinking, *I can do it all. I can be a success in business and still be the husband, father, and friend I want to be.*

Todd and I struggled with his desire to maintain a

balance in reality—not just *saying* other areas in life outside of work were important, but actually *living* as though non-work matters *really* mattered. How could we make that happen?

Sometimes I'd get angry when the pendulum swung too far over on the work side for too long and the family side was neglected. When I'd bring up the problem to Todd, he'd get down on himself. "I'm just a jerk, and I'm not really handling things right." For a while he'd make a conscious effort to be home more and to leave his work at the office—not just literally, but mentally as well. But it was difficult for Todd to disconnect, even when he was at home with me or out in the yard playing with the boys.

For the first five years of our marriage, Todd was so driven to be successful, he could never completely walk away from his work. He took his computer with us wherever we went. His cell phone even came to the beach so he could talk to business clients while he was supposedly relaxing on vacation with the family.

"Hey, wait a minute," I'd say. "That makes the kids and me feel that we're only good enough after you're through with all your phone calls."

"Oh, sorry, Lisa. You know I don't feel that way."

"I know you don't feel that way, Todd, but it sure feels that way to me."

Then, in June of Todd's 30th year, he finally closed the huge deal he'd always dreamed about. For a few weeks, he was elated. I'd find him grinning and knew exactly what he was thinking about. But several weeks later, after the warm glow from the slaps on the back had worn off and the boisterous accolades had faded to stilted silence, he was back to having to perform again in a "what have you done lately" world. Todd realized that making the money was wonderful but not ultimately satisfying. Now the pressure to perform was even greater; he had to work harder in an attempt to top his latest deal. The stress on both of us increased commensurately.

One of the most stressful times occurred a few months later, in October 1999, shortly before Drew was born. During the last few months of my pregnancy, Todd was gone from home almost every night, every week. He was traveling back and forth to North Carolina, where he had a customer with whom he was determined to land a large deal. Todd was doing everything he could to make that client happy.

"I have to be there, Lisa," Todd told me. "I have to go down there and make this deal happen."

He wasn't willing to listen to any alternatives. He didn't want to try to do some of the work by conference call, and to give up the account was unthinkable!

For the first time since I had known Todd, he was extremely off track. He had always been a man of good judgment and wisdom far beyond his years, but now he was making decisions that were simply foolish. One weekend that October, Todd had just returned from being away all week. When he told me he was leaving again and would be away all week, I exploded.

"This is not the way I want to live my life, and I don't think it's the way you want to live yours. Your priorities are totally out of whack. You need to go somewhere and evaluate why you're doing what you're doing!"

Todd left, angry, and I felt awful. I knew I hadn't handled my anger well; nor had I truly communicated my heart to Todd—that I loved him and needed him to be with us more.

That was our pattern: I'd want to talk with Todd about his travel and work schedule, but he was already packing up for the next trip. So I'd yell at him, and he'd retreat into silence, sulking. *A lot of good that did!* I'd think. So this time I decided to try a different approach. One day while David took a nap, I sat down and e-mailed Todd. I included a survey concerning our expectations and desires when it came to balancing work and home. "Fill this out," I said, "and we'll talk about it when you get home."

The survey included such questions as:

- How many nights do you want to be home for dinner per week?
- How many hours are you going to spend working at home each night or on the weekend?
- How many nights are you going to be away, on the average, each month?
- How many days are you going to spend on vacation?
- How often are you going to call home when you're on the road?
- What sort of things are you going to do if your schedule demands last-minute changes?
- How far in advance are you going to inform me of your travel schedule?

I tried to make the survey very tangible. I knew we couldn't deal with everything, but I felt if we could fix some of the little things, we'd both be a lot happier.

By the time Todd came home, he had filled out his survey, and I had filled out mine. It was incredibly reveal-ing to compare our answers. For instance, he said he should be home three nights a week; I said I thought he should be home four. We agreed on three. As it turned out, the survey was something Todd could wrap his arms around. Now he had a gauge by which he could measure himself, a target to shoot at, rather than the nebulous concept of trying to be a better husband and father.

We did something similar with each question. Some of Todd's solutions caused me to smile and love him even more. For example, he said that if his schedule changed unavoidably, forcing him to be late getting home—or worse yet, to miss a family event—he would fine himself, with the money going into an account for family vacations!

As we worked down through the survey, it became apparent to Todd and me that there were larger, overriding issues that caused Todd to feel compelled to work so hard and to derive so much of his self-worth from his job. What were they? And how could we deal with them? In an effort to sort those things out, Todd agreed to set up some sessions with the professional counselor on staff at our church. But even that became part of our dilemma. Now Todd had to find a time to meet with the counselor!

Everything came to a head that fall, when the customer for whom Todd had been bending over backwards called Todd's boss and asked that someone else be put on the account. They wanted somebody in-house who was there on the spot rather than having Todd fly in for a few days at a time.

To me it was an answer to prayer, but Todd's confidence was blown to bits. He was devastated. He'd been trying so hard, yet his best hadn't been good enough. For a performance-oriented, go-to guy who was used to making things happen, that failure was a huge blow to his pride. It took a while for him to realize that the deal falling through was actually a blessing—a turning point in our marriage and in our outlook on life.

Todd and I scheduled a "retreat day" at a park, where the two of us could go to a relaxed setting and talk about what we were doing, why we were doing it, and what we wanted our life to look like. It was a defining time for both of us. We wanted to reset our course by a true compass rather than one that was slightly off-kilter. Todd later said, "I began to realize that no matter how much I want to do things right for my customer, sometimes it's out of my control. I can do all the right things, and it still may not work out the way I had hoped. For me to sacrifice those things most precious to me—my family and my relationship with God—for something that doesn't matter just doesn't make any sense."

After the deal fell through in October, an amazing sense of freedom washed over Todd and me. Life around the Beamer place was much more relaxed as we approached the birth of our second baby in February. When Drew was born, Todd was around a lot. He found ways to work out of his home office so he could have more time with the boys and me.

We were making progress, but real change didn't happen overnight. After Drew was born, Todd and I realized more than ever that we really were on the same page when it came to what we wanted out of life. The key was first establishing realistic expectations and then doing whatever it took to make the priorities we committed to actually happen. It helped Todd immensely to realize there were some areas he *could* change, that he wasn't bound to doing things the way he'd done them in the past. Perhaps most of all, Todd saw the truth: "This is real life right now. I'm not going to start living it after I accomplish a few more goals or get a few more dollars in the bank. I'm living today. My wife and kids are here right now, so I don't want to say, 'I'll just keep up this schedule until something cataclysmic happens, and then I'll be the person I want to be.' This is the only shot I have, so I better find out what's most important and then do it."

Eventually Todd even made it to a few sessions with the counselor at church and talked about some of the reasons he felt so driven to succeed. He came away with a renewed awareness that his self-esteem didn't depend on financial success or success in his career. It was based on the simple truth that God created him with intrinsic worth, and that regardless of how he performed, God loved him and valued him as *Todd*—not as a computer-software supersalesman, or as the world's greatest husband, father, and friend, or even as a super-spiritual person.

As Todd and I both came to understand more about God's grace, we realized we didn't have to be perfect for God to love us. We didn't always have to have all the right answers. We didn't always have to perform perfectly. It may seem simple to some people, but for us, that was truly a liberating spiritual revelation!

Change came slowly, but it did come. No longer did Todd have a success-at-all-costs mentality. Earlier in his career he often said, "Lisa, I really don't have a choice. I have to work late; I must be at that meeting."

But as we talked through those kinds of issues now, I gently reminded him, "No, you're not a slave, Todd. You can make choices."

"I'll take that under advisement," Todd would say with a sly smile. He normally internalized my assessments, processed them for a while, and then chose his family over his work.

Oh, he still had his cell phones, his computer, and his Palm Pilot as his security blankets. But every once in a while I'd notice a note on his normally "business dates only" Palm Pilot such as, "Send Lisa flowers," or "Lunch with the boys." More importantly, Todd set an alarm in the Palm Pilot that went off at 5:30 P.M. each day as a reminder to start wrapping up his work so he could spend sufficient time in the evening with the boys and me. Todd no longer just talked about how much he loved us; he *showed* us.

In tangible ways, Todd took his new priorities to heart. He was offered a coveted management position at Oracle but turned it down so he could have more control of his schedule. Like any corporate business, Oracle is an extremely competitive environment, and eliciting strong commitments from its employees is part of the company's success. Todd was still a go-the-extra-mile type of employee. But for the first time he began setting boundaries around our home life that not even his job could encroach upon or tempt him to cross.

Todd especially appreciated the encouragement he received from the Friday-morning breakfast guys, who challenged him to maintain proper balance in his life. He gained great insights from *The Seven Seasons of a Man's Life* by Patrick Morley, a book the group used to stimulate discussions. In it, Morley asserts:

> Men may work too hard because of fear, because of their values, because they selfishly enjoy work, or because they hope to escape conflict in their home. They may still be seeking to win the approval of their own fathers. Whatever the reason, it is not rational.[2]

Todd underlined the statement and then numbered his top personal reasons for working so hard. He placed fear in the number one spot. Second, he truly enjoyed his work, and third, he wanted to please his father.

Fear of failure was definitely Todd's nemesis; he wanted to know that he was the best. He wanted to win and usually did, whether it was a Ping-Pong game at his grandmother's home, a church softball game, or his work. And he loved to work! To Todd, his job wasn't drudgery. He looked forward to getting up and going out to work each day. He enjoyed what he did so much that it was easy for him to get carried away with it. "I need to make some calls," he'd say, going into his office. "I'll be about a half hour."

Forty-five minutes to an hour later, I'd have to go tap on his door. "Todd, time's up." Sometimes I'd tell David to go

[2]Patrick M. Morley, *The Seven Seasons of a Man's Life* (Grand Rapids, Mich.: Zondervan Publishing House, 1997), 79.

get Daddy from his office when he'd been in there too long. David would say, "Pack it up, Dad!" And Todd would!

Todd's dad, too, was successful in his career. Although Todd wasn't competitive with his dad, in his mind his father was the model of the success Todd had originally sought. He drew inspiration from his father and enjoyed proving to his dad that he could close the big deal.

What made Todd different from many workaholics was that he recognized his temptations and took steps to avoid them. He pulled the "success monkey" off his back and pitched it. Then he picked up on another Morley principle and used it as a measuring stick to help keep his work in check and his priorities in order: "Failure means to succeed in a way that doesn't really matter."[3] It was the last book Todd would ever work through with the breakfast group, and it may have been the most important.

■ ■ ■ ■

Over the Christmas and New Year's holidays in 1999 we visited, as we normally did, with both Todd's family and my family. While with my family, just for fun, each of us wrote out an assessment of where we were in our lives, our goals for the coming year, and our long-term goals for the next 10, 20, and 30 years. Todd wrote that in 20 years he planned to be president of his own company, Beamer Enterprises, living on a lake in North Carolina and working out of our home. In 30 years he wanted to be executive vice president of operations of a company that he and my youn-

[3]Morley, 84.

135

ger brother, Jonathan, would start: Brosious Enterprises. He predicted we'd have three children by 2010 and six grandchildren by 2030.

It was great fun to write out our goals for the future. We even created a time capsule that we planned to open on New Year's Eve, 2010. Each of us placed in the capsule our predictions for the future and some personal items of interest. For instance, I put in a prediction that Todd and I would have three children and still be living in New Jersey. The biggest change in the world, I said, would be the regulation of the telemarketing industry so there would be no more annoying telemarketing calls at home during dinner.

Each of us put in the time capsule some things indicative of our life as it was in the 1990s. For our family, we put in a church bulletin; I put in a disposable diaper, a grocery receipt, and a baby-names book. As representative of his life in the late 1990s, Todd contributed an Oracle shirt and a cell phone. The cell phone was considered state-of-the-art technology at the end of the 20th century, and we looked forward to comparing it with the latest and greatest gizmos to come in the future.

We also wrote out a few of our favorite things. Todd's musical favorites were Tim McGraw, Alan Jackson, and Garth Brooks. His favorite songs: "(I've Got) Friends in Low Places" and "The Dance."

His favorite movie was *A River Runs Through It*. Todd and I had seen the movie while we were dating, shortly after a friend's father had died. Todd hadn't experienced death close-up before. Although as an 11-year-old he'd seen his mom grieve over her cousin, Jerry Workman, who had died at age 41, death hadn't yet touched anyone closer in his life. But as Todd observed his roommate dealing with his dad's death, he was moved to tears.

A River Runs Through It revolves around the relationship of two brothers—one of whom dies—and a dad. Todd saw the movie several times, and each time it brought tears to his eyes as he recognized the importance of quality relationships and the fragility of life.

Maybe that's why, when we wrote out what we should do more of, Todd wrote, "Spend more time with the kids and Lisa."

The year 2000 was upon us. It was the end of an era, and some people said it was the beginning of a new millennium . . . depending, of course, how you chose to calculate it. We laughed a lot and made humorous comments as we deposited our items in the time capsule. I had a weird feeling as we were doing it. It occurred to me that, quite possibly, one of us could die before we opened the time capsule. I wasn't being morbid, just thinking realistically. I didn't say anything as I glanced across the room toward my precious mom, the most likely candidate. Then I shook my head, snapping back to the joyful celebration. But the thought continued to nag at me: *I wonder if one of us won't be here. . . .*

12

LIVING THE DREAM

WE BEGAN BUILDING our dream house in 2000—well, at least it was a dream house to us! Our older home in Hightstown had served us well, but now with two growing boys, we wanted more space and a yard where the kids could play safely. We found a piece of property in Cranbury, New Jersey, just 10 minutes or so from our old house, and built a spacious new home with an open floor plan, lots of windows, and a basement that Todd wanted and I didn't.

"We *need* a basement," Todd overdramatized as we were laying out the plans for our home.

"Why do we need a basement, Todd? It's just a place to collect junk."

"Exactly! And where else are you going to put all that junk if you don't have a basement?"

Finally I gave up. "Okay, Todd, if you want a basement, we can have one." *It's going to be under the house anyhow,* I thought. *Why should I care? I'll never go down there.*

We built the basement, and sure enough, Todd was right. We needed the basement, although I never could have anticipated the sort of collections we'd accumulate down there.

We moved in to our new home in the summer of 2000. Not only did Todd get his basement, he got his "Beamer room"—a home office where he could retreat from the world—as well. The kids got a backyard, complete with a wooden fort and swing set. Me? I got a spacious kitchen—a place where our family could eat, talk, and laugh. It had hardwood floors and a sunroom, complete with fresh flowers and wicker furniture, where I could sit and enjoy a quiet moment now and then.

When Todd asked my mom, a talented artist, if she'd come and paint a mural on one section of his office wall, she gladly consented.

Since he was a successful businessman with an appreciation for the finer things in life, one might expect Todd to request some esoteric scene on his office wall . . . something that might aptly connote the erudite side of his personality.

Nope. Not Todd. He asked my mom to paint a mural of Michael Jordan's final scoring shot as a member of the Chicago Bulls. And Mom did it! There, on Todd's office wall, is a wonderful rendition of Michael midair, in full Bulls regalia, wearing number 23 and tossing up the final basket of his Bulls career, with a crowd of Chicago fans looking on. Mom even added a special touch just for Todd. Down along the front row, to the right of the backboard, she painted in four familiar faces—Todd, David, Drew, and me. We weren't actually in attendance that night, but it sure felt as though we were when we saw Mom's painting.

We loved our new home, especially being able to sit

outside on a summer night, after the boys were in bed, and hear nothing but quiet. It was on one of those nights that we had a conversation about how good our life was and how fortunate we were—not only because we had material comforts but because we were rich in life's intangibles. We were deeply in love; we had weathered the storm over his work schedule versus our family time; and we were thriving physically, emotionally, and spiritually. We had developed a deep trust in each other, as well as a willingness to be vulnerable with one another.

We had two wonderful boys and a great extended family. We took fun vacations, including camping trips with the boys to Cape Cod, the Catskill Mountains, and North Carolina. We had caring friends and a warmhearted church in which we took an active part. Truth is, we were fabulously rich! Life couldn't have been any better!

■ ■ ■ ■

In June 2001, Todd and I found out we were expecting another baby. We had always hoped for three children— someday—but this pregnancy was something of a surprise. Our third child was due in mid-January 2002. When we told David that we were going to have another baby, he pointed at Drew and said, "Why? We already have one!"

■ ■ ■ ■

That summer found Todd working on another goal, only this one involved the boys and me. He wanted to take the boys to every Major League Baseball stadium in the country. We got off to a good start during the summer of 2001, attending games at Shea Stadium and Yankee Stadium in New York, and Oriole Park at Camden Yards in Baltimore.

My family loved the Yankees and Todd loved the Cubs, but for some reason we couldn't explain, our son David developed an affinity for the New York Mets. We went to Shea Stadium for the Mets-Cubs game on July 4, and the Mets drubbed the Cubs. Although it went against his team loyalties, Todd bought David a Mets batting helmet.

David was ecstatic! He teased Todd all the way home, "My Mets beat your Cubs, Dad! My Mets beat your Cubs!"

We kept busy throughout the summer of 2001, going to Cape Cod in August, as well as to Todd's grandparents' anniversary party at his Aunt Bonnie and Uncle Rick's home in Washington, D.C. At first Todd's older sister, Melissa, and her husband, Greg, didn't think they could make the weekend trip all the way from their home in Michigan. But Todd called and told them, "You have to come. I've already arranged tickets for you using my frequent-flier miles." So Melissa and Greg rearranged their plans and came.

It was the first time in eight years that all the adult members of the Beamer family were together with no children to distract our conversations. In retrospect, it's easy to see now that the get-together was providentially arranged.

On August 24, on the way down to the party, we

stopped in Baltimore to see the Orioles. The great Cal Ripken had announced his retirement from baseball at the end of the season, and Todd wanted to see Cal play one last time. As I watched Todd, David, and Drew walking in front of me toward the entrance of Oriole Park, I felt compelled to take a picture of the scene. It was a great shot of the three of them, hand in hand, excited about spending a few hours together at a ball game. I could never have imagined what a treasure that picture would become to our family.

The following weekend, on September 1, we visited Keith and Sandy Franz and their children at their home in Elizabethtown, Pennsylvania. While the guys played Wiffle ball with the kids in the backyard, Sandy and I sat on the back patio, talking about my current pregnancy.

"Are you excited about having another baby, Lisa?" Sandy asked.

"Actually, I am," I replied. I gazed at Todd and Keith, laughing and playing ball with the kids. "Todd is such a great father. As soon as he walks through the door from work, the boys go ballistic! 'Daddy's home!' They just love him. Todd doesn't do the things a father is supposed to do just *because* he's supposed to; he does them because he truly loves our children."

As we packed up to leave later that evening, we told Keith and Sandy we'd be out of town next week because we were going to Rome on an Oracle reward trip. Todd thought it would be terrific if Keith and Sandy could go with us on one of our excursions. "We need to get together more often," Todd insisted. "These 24-hour trips are too short. We ought to go on vacation together sometime."

■ ■ ■ ■

Back home, Todd was about to begin a Body for Life diet
and exercise program with our friend Doug MacMillan.
Lately Todd had been feeling self-conscious about his
weight. He was a big guy, about six feet tall, so his normal
college "playing weight" was around 180. But recently he
had been tipping the scales at nearly 200 pounds. He looked
and felt great, and he was still active playing on the church
softball team, but he'd lost a bit of the muscle tone he'd
once enjoyed as an athlete. "I've got to get back in shape,"
he lamented when he noticed some pudginess in the bathroom mirror.

A few months earlier he'd discovered the Body for Life
program when a college friend e-mailed pictures of himself
before and after using it. Todd was impressed with the
results and decided to get the book and take the challenge.
He thought it would be an excellent 12-week regimen. It
was perfect for someone like Todd—someone who liked to
deal with spreadsheets, specific goals, and monitored
results. He wanted an orderly and disciplined approach to
getting in shape.

Todd was really excited about this new program. In
fact, prior to our trip to Rome, he had made up all sorts of
spreadsheets listing his daily exercises and thoroughly
planning his eating and exercise regime, including recipes
for meals that he could eat (which he gave to me to
prepare). Todd and Doug had planned to begin their diet
and exercise program earlier that summer, but since we
were away from home so much, it was difficult to main-

tain any consistency. Something always came up to inter-fere.

"Okay," Todd announced. "We'll be away a lot during the summer, so I'll start the first week in September."

"Todd, we're going to Rome that week! You don't want to start dieting right before we go on vacation," I teased. "Set yourself up for success. Why not start after we get back?"

"Good idea," Todd said. "I'll tell ya what. We'll be in Rome during the first week of September, so once I get home, I'll start the new diet. Let's see, I'll start on . . . September 11."

ROMAN HOLIDAY

"Todd, you are *not* taking that computer along with us to Rome."

"Yes, I am."

"No, you're not!"

"But I might need to contact someone—"

"Todd, we're going on vacation . . . holiday . . . rest . . . relaxation . . . fun . . . remember?"

It was our normal prevacation "fight," with Todd struggling to disconnect from work and me trying to make sure he did! Neither of us took this fight too seriously anymore; it had almost gotten to the point of being humorous. The good news was that Todd had grown accustomed to my last-minute "security" checks, and usually he was willing to leave the computer behind. He just needed me to remind him.

"Okay, okay," he finally conceded, "but it's going to be a long night when we get home. I'll have to get all my work ready for the San Francisco trip on Monday evening."

I nodded, but I didn't dare appear too sympathetic

toward Todd's plight or he'd wrap his arms around that computer bag again.

We set off for Rome along with about 500 other Oracle employees and guests, including Stan and Kathleen Ueland and Jonathan and Jana Oomrigar. Stan had lived next door to Todd at Wheaton College, and he and Kathleen had married shortly after graduation. Todd had helped Stan get his foot in the door at Oracle and had quietly checked in with him ever since, giving advice whenever Stan asked and watching out for him as a big brother. I'd never met Kathleen before, but she was pregnant with their second child, so we had a lot in common.

Jonathan Oomrigar worked in Oracle's California office and was one of Todd's favorite people with the company. I had never met the Oomrigars, but I'd heard many stories of Jonathan and Todd's "exploits" on some of their business trips together to Israel, Tokyo, and all over the United States. One of their favorite stories was about the time they were at a formal, traditional Japanese business dinner in Tokyo. They had to sit on the floor for hours, and at the conclusion of the dinner, having lost nearly all feeling in his legs, Todd got up slowly. But when he bent over to put on his shoes, he split his suit pants. Undoubtedly he made quite an impression on his Japanese hosts!

The Oracle trips always combined business with pleasure, so along with the other Oracle reps, we convened for special company dinners each night while in Rome. During the days we were on our own, so the Oomrigars joined us as we explored various parts of the city, including a visit to the Vatican.

During my spare time while in Rome, I was reading about the book of Esther in the Bible. I was scheduled to lead a study on the subject at church when we returned home. Esther, a young Jewish woman, became queen of Persia. Because of her position and background, she was used by God to help deliver her people, the Jews, from a sinister plot to destroy them. A pivotal point in the story came when Esther's relative, Mordecai, challenged her to use the position she had obtained for good. He confronted her with a strong admonition that God could—and would—find someone else to fill her role if she refused to act courageously and confront the evil situation. "If you keep quiet at a time like this, God will deliver the Jews from some other source, but you and your relatives will die. What's more, who can say but that God has brought you into the palace for just such a time as this?"[4]

At the risk of her life, Esther stepped up and did the right thing. As a result, the evil plot was exposed, the perpetrators were punished, and Esther's people were saved. The main theme of the story is that God is in charge, and he sometimes uses us for good in circumstances we would never have chosen of our own volition.

As I read over my study guide on Esther's story, I came to a suggested Bible memory passage for the first week. To my surprise, it was Romans 11:33-36, the exact verses of Scripture that had come to mean so much to me after my dad's death. *This is great,* I thought as I read over the passage. *I don't even have to memorize this. I already know it:*

[4]See Esther 4:14.

Oh, the depth of the riches of the wisdom and knowledge
   of God!
How unsearchable his judgments,
and his paths beyond tracing out!
"Who has known the mind of the Lord?
Or who has been his counselor?"
"Who has ever given to God,
that God should repay him?"
For from him and through him and to him are all things.
To him be the glory forever! Amen.

These were the words I was to focus on as I prepared to teach the lesson when we returned home, the week of September 10. It wasn't until later that I realized why God had brought those words to the forefront of my mind again.

■　■　■　■

On Saturday, September 8, Todd and I took a day trip to Florence, once the home of such creative writers and artists as Dante, Leonardo da Vinci, and Michelangelo. When we visited the famous marble statue of David, completed by Michelangelo in 1504, Todd bought a small replica of the statue to take home for our son David. "David's gonna love this!" Todd beamed.

Besides its museums, art galleries, ornate architecture, and ancient statuary, Florence is also known as a jewelry lover's paradise. Todd and I stopped to browse at a small jewelry store along one of the side streets, where I spotted a beautiful diamond tennis bracelet. "If you're ever looking for a special gift for me . . . ," I said with a smile.

I'd always wanted a diamond tennis bracelet, and this one was rather unusual, with diamonds set in flowers made of white gold. It was gorgeous . . . and I loved it. But Todd and I didn't spend that sort of money on a whim. Besides, we had no way of knowing for sure if the bracelet was worth the price the shop owners were asking.

"Well, should we buy it?" Todd asked.

"Oh, I don't know . . . ," I debated.

I could see Todd's practical side kicking into gear, and I could guess what he was thinking. *How do we know these are real stones? How can we be sure this is real gold? What if we get it back home and have it appraised, only to discover we've been ripped off?*

We went back and forth about the bracelet.

"Do you like it?" Todd asked.

"I love it!"

"Do you think we should get it?"

"I don't know."

"Yeah, I wonder if those diamonds are real. They look great under the shop owner's scope, but I can't tell for sure, can you?"

"It sure is beautiful. . . ."

"I'll bet that's not even real white gold. . . ."

"It looks good on. . . ."

We bantered back and forth for nearly half an hour about the merits and risks of buying the bracelet. "I really don't want to be taken advantage of here," Todd whispered to me out of the clerk's earshot.

He wasn't being stingy or cheap—he'd bought me beautiful diamond earrings for our fifth anniversary. No, Todd wanted assurance that the bracelet was authentic and that it was a good deal. Finally I said, "Todd, it is what it is. There's no way we'll know for sure if this is a good deal. We're not going to know more than we know right now. We don't have anyone whose appraisal we can depend on. If you don't want to do it, that's okay with me. If you do, you'll just have to take it on faith."

We bought the bracelet.

It was so out of character for us, yet we did it. Today, that bracelet is one of my most cherished possessions . . . and I've never had it appraised! It may be costume jewelry for all I know, but to me it's priceless.

■　■　■　■

On Sunday Todd and I viewed the ruins around Rome, including the Colosseum, the ancient Roman amphitheater where many early Christians were slaughtered by lions or gladiators. It was hard to imagine men being so cruel to other human beings, but it was a grim reminder of the price many men and women have paid for the faith and freedom we take for granted.

Todd was especially fascinated by the ruins from an architectural standpoint. He was impressed that the people of ancient Rome could have built such incredible structures without the aid of our modern construction equipment and technology.

We took a break from sight-seeing to enjoy some pizza

Todd, ready to see the world in his stroller
Flint, MI, 1969

Trying to look as big as sister Melissa
Flint, MI, 1972

Poised for a home run
Glen Ellyn, IL, 1978

Mom and Dad
Brosious with Lisa,
just before church
Albany, NY, 1969

Lisa, Holly, and Paul,
dressed for Halloween in
Mom's homemade costumes
Peekskill, NY, 1975

Dad, Lisa, and
Tatsy the cat
Shrub Oak, NY, 1979

Addressing the
graduates at
his high school,
Wheaton Academy
Wheaton, IL, 1986

Keith Franz, Stan
Ueland, and Todd,
back from waterskiing
Littleton, NC, 1989

Todd, Keith Franz,
and Dave Rockness
in their Wheaton
College apartment
Wheaton, IL, 1991

Todd and his
new briefcase, all
business on college
graduation day
Wheaton, IL, 1991

Todd, safely "home"
Wheaton, IL, 1991

Grace Hutter, Pam Hill, Kara Lundstrom, Lisa, Sandy Oyler, and Stacey Shrader at college graduation
Wheaton, IL, 1991

Falling in love (with Michael Jordan looking on!)
Wheaton, IL, 1992

Working hard at Wilson Sporting Goods
Rosemont, IL, 1992

A Beamer Christmas in California: Dad, Coco, Todd,
Mom, Greg (Melissa's husband), Melissa, and Michele
Los Gatos, CA, 1993

Paul, Todd, Lisa, Jonathan, and Holly after a long hike
New Paltz, NY, 1993

Lisa and Janet Odland,
15 years into our friendship
Shrub Oak, NY, 1993

Getting engaged on
Turkey Mountain
Yorktown, NY, 1993

Moving to New Jersey
Iselin, NJ, 1994

Todd and Lisa *Beamer*,
for the first time!
Peekskill, NY, 1994

Paula Daniels, Joe Urbanowicz,
and Lisa celebrate our wedding
Peekskill, NY, 1994

Finally off for
our honeymoon
New York, NY, 1994

Todd's first trip to the top of
the Empire State Building
New York, NY, 1994

First apartment and
first Christmas together
Princeton, NJ, 1994

Our favorite vacation ever—Yellowstone National Park
Yellowstone, WY, 1995

Enjoying our five-year
reunion at Wheaton College
Wheaton, IL, 1996

Finding the perfect
Christmas tree, a
Thanksgiving tradition
Red Hook, NY, 1996

The proud dad with
a brand-new David
Somerville, NJ, 1998

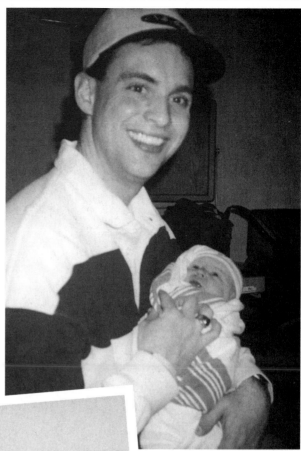

Daddy and David tune
in to the Super Bowl
(who cares that the
Bears weren't playing!)
Hightstown, NJ, 1999

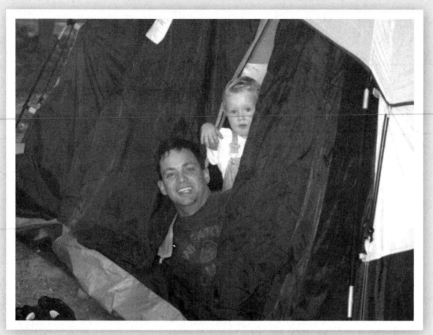

First camping trip for David and for Daddy
(Mom had a lot of teaching to do)
Phoenicia, NY, 1999

Daddy and David celebrating America at our town's
Memorial Day parade
Hightstown, NJ, 1999

The Beamer
boys welcome
another—Drew!
Hamilton, NJ, 2000

Drew's dedication at Princeton Alliance Church
Plainsboro, NJ, 2000

Christmas memories
New York, NY, 2000

Father's Day
with two
adoring fans
Cranbury, NJ, 2001

Golfing with the Friday-morning guys: Doug MacMillan, Axel Johnson,
George Pittas, Todd, Tony McAnaney, John Edgar Caterson
Ocean City, MD, 2001

Exploring
the ruins
Rome, Italy,
September 8, 2001

Our last night
in Rome
Rome, Italy,
September 9, 2001

Memories of Todd,
left at the crash site
Shanksville, PA,
September 17, 2001

Michele, Lisa,
and Melissa
reflect at the site
*Shanksville, PA,
September 17, 2001*

Morgan and Mom, ready
to go home from the hospital
Princeton, NJ, January 11, 2002

David, Drew, Mom, and
Morgan, celebrating Easter
Shrub Oak, NY, March 31, 2002

at a street-side café, and then later cooled off with chocolate gelato cones as we sat by a fountain. Despite the magnificent beauty of Italy, our favorite part of the trip was the gelato. We had at least one serving each day on this trip. Looking back, it seems only fitting that Todd got to enjoy a chocolate binge that week. I'm glad he did!

We took lots of pictures, mostly of Todd in front of ruins, and returned to our hotel that afternoon, tired but happy. Oracle hosted a black-tie dinner that night. It was a beautiful evening and a lovely way to end the trip. Todd and I said our good-byes to the others, then retired to our room while the party was still going on because we had an early flight the next day.

We left Rome at four o'clock Monday morning and tried our best to relax during the all-day transatlantic flight. Although Todd was dressed casually in sweatpants, T-shirt, and baseball hat, I could tell he was already disconnecting from "vacation mode." The wheels were turning in his mind concerning what he had to do when we got home and during the workweek ahead.

As we were now in the habit of doing, we discussed Todd's travel plans and his schedule, especially his upcoming trip to San Francisco. The trip had looked much more innocuous prior to our trip to Rome; now, on board the jet headed for home, the overnight trip seemed rather daunting.

Todd had an important meeting with representatives from the Sony Corporation, for whom he was working on a major project. He was scheduled to take an early flight out of Newark Tuesday morning and arrive on the West Coast around noon. He had a 1:00 P.M. meeting scheduled in San

Francisco that day and a dinner meeting that night, after which he was planning to take the red-eye flight back home.

When he'd first mentioned the whirlwind trip, I'd flinched. But I knew this trip was an aberration rather than the norm. For the past couple of years, Todd and I had been doing extremely well on our communication about work responsibilities and priorities. Ordinarily I would have challenged him to rethink the possibilities, looking for alternatives, when something came up that didn't make rational sense or was such a severe strain on Todd.

At the very least I'd inquire, "Why are you doing this? What are the alternatives? Do you really need to be at that meeting? Could you reschedule at a better time?" Todd appreciated my challenges, and often just thinking through the options saved us both a lot of hassles.

But concerning his trip on September 11, I didn't grill him, partly because I knew that someone else had called the meeting unexpectedly, and partly because I didn't want to bug Todd about it while we were on vacation. Beyond that, I knew that the meeting was important—that the Sony executives were flying in from Japan, the CFO of Oracle was attending, and it was totally out of Todd's hands to reschedule it.

"When are you going to be home this week?" I asked.

"Oh, this is going to be a really bad week," Todd said softly. "I just can't wait for the weekend. I wish it were Saturday right now."

Todd's statement took me by surprise. We had already made plans for that weekend to go bike-riding with the boys in a nearby state park. I knew Todd was looking forward to that, but he was usually extremely positive and enthusiastic about work, even when challenges loomed.

"I just can't wait to get through this week," Todd said again, almost as much to himself as to me. "I have a lot on my plate for the next couple of days. . . ."

Neither of us had any idea how prophetic—or under-stated—his words were.

14

A WHIRLWIND
ARRIVAL—AND
DEPARTURE

WE LANDED AT Newark International Airport in mid-afternoon on September 10. It was a bright, beautiful day as our plane touched down. However, by the time we cleared customs, retrieved our car from the airport parking lot, and drove 45 minutes north to meet my mom and our boys, the skies had turned ominous. It was pouring down rain.

We met Mom, David, and Drew halfway between her home and ours, at our usual meeting spot, a rest area along the parkway. There was little opportunity for small talk since enormous drops of rain were soaking all of us. Also, since our flight had been late, Mom was in a hurry; she had to get back to work.

"How was the trip?" she called as Todd and I hurriedly carried the boys and their belongings from her car to our minivan, buckling the boys into their car seats.

"It was great!" Todd called back to her.

We waved a quick good-bye, clambered into the minivan, and tried to dry off. We all figured we'd have plenty of time to catch up with each other in a few days, when things settled back down to normal.

Todd had considered landing in Newark and then flying on to San Francisco on September 10. But he'd decided to come home first so he could spend at least one night with the boys before getting back on a plane.

Ironically, it seemed we had made the right decision, since a construction fire late Monday afternoon at Newark International had shut down the airport for a while that evening, canceling the flight Todd had thought of taking.

Although we didn't know it at the time, another young father had rearranged his flight plans as well. His evening flight was canceled due to the fire, so he booked the next available flight to San Francisco: United Flight 93, leaving from Newark at 8:00 A.M. on Tuesday morning. The young man's name was Jeremy Glick.

■   ■   ■   ■

It was five o'clock in the evening when we finally stepped inside our home. Mom had made a meal for us—one of Todd's favorites—meat loaf, macaroni and cheese, and a fresh-baked pie. I really appreciated her thoughtfulness, as I had cleaned out all the perishables before leaving for vacation, and we had hardly any food to eat in the refrigerator. *Mom always takes good care of the boys,* I thought as I smiled to myself and put the food in the oven to warm up.

Todd unloaded the suitcases from the car and hauled them upstairs for me to deal with after dinner. He knew I liked to unpack the first night we got home, so when I woke up the next morning with the boys, I wouldn't have to deal with the mess of dirty clothes in suitcases.

It was going to be a busy week for me, too.

David was scheduled to start preschool on Wednesday, Drew was going to Gymboree classes, and my Bible study was starting Thursday. Whew! What more could we pack into this week?

Todd had no sooner put down the suitcases and bounded down the stairs than he was rolling on the floor, playing with the boys. Squeals of delight filled our home; in the blink of an eye the boys' playroom floor was nearly covered with toys. Todd and the boys were having a ball!

Todd had searched all over Rome to find a soccer shirt with the number 6, David's favorite number. He couldn't find one, but he did find some shirts with the names of European soccer players on the back. One player's name was *Davids*. So David's shirt was *Davids,* number 26. Todd also found some matching red jerseys for the boys so they could pretend they were on the same team.

David's and Drew's shirts hung down around their legs like nightshirts, but they didn't seem to mind. Drew, who was just beginning to speak in real words, couldn't really express his thanks to Todd in sentences. But the smile on his face said it all.

"We're on the same team now," David told his little brother.

We also bought a little wooden train for Drew with his name on it. Drew likes trains, and he especially enjoyed getting something David didn't!

Todd also gave David the small replica of the famous

sculpture of King David we'd seen in Florence. David looked at it quizzically, as though to say, "What's this naked guy all about, Dad?"

Todd tried to explain. "You know, *David?* The guy in the Bible who killed the giant Goliath with just a little pebble?"

David knew the Bible story well. He just couldn't figure out what this porcelain guy with no clothes on had to do with any of it.

Todd gently plucked the statue out of David's hands. "Well, okay, we'll just put that away for a few years. . . ."

After supper I said to Todd, "Tell you what. You take the boys upstairs and give them a bath while I do the dishes and clean up the kitchen."

"Sounds good to me," Todd replied. He loved to help the boys get their baths. Usually he came out of the bathroom more soaked than the kids.

When we arrived home that night, our friend Doug MacMillan was at our house. Known as the resident handyman among the Friday-morning breakfast group, Doug could fix almost anything. His motto was "You guys break it, and I'll fix it." He enjoyed taking odd jobs and had been working to install a tile backsplash over the kitchen countertop while were away in Italy. He had hoped to finish the job before we returned but hadn't quite been able to.

Doug often teased Todd about his ineptitude when it came to carpentry or other household repairs. Doug liked to joke that when he opened Todd's toolbox, he found a piece of paper with Doug's phone number written on it. As he and Todd talked in the kitchen, Todd noticed that Doug had pulled one of the wall plugs out of the enclosure while he tiled around it, and it was hanging in midair—still connected to the electricity.

"Do you want this put back in the wall?" Todd asked as he grabbed the box on both sides.

Doug waited a few seconds before answering, knowing full well that the current was still on and Todd was holding a "live" electrical box. He knew there was little danger of Todd being hurt, but Doug also knew that by grabbing the box the way Todd had, the circuit was completed and Todd was no doubt getting quite a buzz.

"Kinda tingles, doesn't it?" Doug finally deadpanned.

Todd slowly released his grip as though nothing was wrong, grinned slightly, and said, "I think I'll let you finish it." Then he headed upstairs to give the boys their baths.

After Todd had tucked the boys into bed and prayed with them, he came back downstairs and made a beeline for his office. Vacation was over; it was time to get back to work. "I have to make some calls about my meetings tomorrow and download all my e-mail," Todd called out to me. Then, just as a little barb, he said, "You know, I wouldn't have to do that if you'd let me take my computer to Rome!"

We both laughed. I was glad he hadn't taken it, and he was, too—though he'd never admit it.

I went upstairs, unpacked our clothes, cleaned up a bit, and got ready for bed. I was dead tired. It was only about 9:00 P.M., but that was nearly 3:00 A.M. in Rome, where we had started the day. I sat down on our bed, but before I crawled beneath the covers, I called my mom.

Mom wanted to hear all about our trip, but I was too

tired to carry on much of a conversation. "Sorry to be in such a rush today," Mom said. "I hardly got a chance to say hi to Todd."

"Oh, don't worry, Mom," I said sleepily. "You'll have lots of time to talk with him the next time you see him."

I said good-bye to Mom and turned out the light. Downstairs I could vaguely hear Doug and Todd talking as I drifted off to sleep.

"I'd be glad to help you, buddy," Todd told Doug, "but I've got to fly out tomorrow morning bright and early for a whirlwind trip to San Francisco."

"Man, Todd, you just got home." Doug's voice revealed both his surprise and his concern. As a member of the Friday group, Doug had prayed with Todd often regarding the balance between his desire to be home with the children and me, and the travel required by his career.

"Yeah, I know," Todd replied. "But I'll be back Wednesday morning."

■ ■ ■ ■

The next morning, Todd awakened early and drove to Newark International. No doubt Todd was in a rush as he raced down the long, glassed-in corridor of Terminal A. Most likely he didn't even notice the four young, Middle Eastern–looking passengers as he hurried past the T.G.I. Friday's restaurant on the left side of the hall to the check-in counter at A-17, and boarded his flight to San Francisco—United Airlines Flight 93.

15

INSIDE THE NIGHTMARE

As I sat on the bed that Tuesday morning, September 11, my world had suddenly come to a halt. For a long time after I saw the crash site on TV and heard the news that it was a United flight that had crashed in Pennsylvania, I stared blankly at the field outside our window, trying to make sense of it all. Just a few short hours earlier, Todd had been lying beside me. Now I was certain he was dead. My day had started out so . . . *ordinary*—with a shower, breakfast, laundry. And then the phone call had come. My mind somehow couldn't reconcile the two realities.

I watched as large birds, some sort of buzzards, swooped down and pecked at something in the weeds. They didn't seem to be in any hurry. It was as though the birds of prey had free reign on this day.

I kept my bedroom door open all day but told our close friends, "If you come into this room, you must be calm. Please, let's not have any hysteria in here." I wasn't trying to be especially noble or stoic. I simply knew that I couldn't handle it emotionally if people around me were losing their composure, so I decided early on that somehow we were going to remain as calm as possible. Apparently our friends passed the word along, because most people who came into the room maintained their composure.

My friend Elaine's husband, Brian, arrived soon after I had gone upstairs, as did our good friend Doug MacMillan. Brian and Doug had been on the phone with all sorts of people, trying to find out any information they could. They had already begun to surmise that Todd had been on United Flight 93. Eventually they reached someone at United Airlines, but United wouldn't confirm anything. "Let us take your number in case we need to get hold of you," United said.

Brian and Doug came in the bedroom and quietly said, "We don't know for sure, but we're pretty sure Todd was on that plane."

"I know," I replied softly.

A while later, Brian returned. "Lisa, Oracle called." He stopped and tried to clear his throat. "Their travel people have confirmed that Todd was booked on that flight."

What to do? What to do?

What *do* you do when your whole world is suddenly turned upside down?

In the midst of the blur, my logical nature went on auto-pilot, reminding me that I needed to be the one to inform those closest to me about the crash. I called my mom first.

I tried to break the news to her gently. "I'm fairly certain Todd was on the flight that went down in Pennsylvania."

"No, that can't be," Mom protested.

"I know it is, Mom."

"I'll pack some clothes and be down there right away."

"Well, you can't get down here right now. The New Jersey Turnpike is closed." In fact, although I didn't know it, all the major highways between New York City and Washington, D.C., had been blocked off to public traffic, as authorities worried about possible terrorist activities in tunnels or on bridges.

Mom said, "I'll get there somehow."

Next I called Todd's mom in Washington, D.C., with the same message. "I'm fairly certain . . ."

Todd's dad was conducting a business meeting—ironically, in San Francisco—so Peggy was all alone. Her voice quivered as she softly asked, "What can we do to confirm it?"

I told her what Brian and Doug had told me. "United is going to call us back, and I'll call you as soon as we know anything."

■   ■   ■   ■

Shortly after noon United Airlines called. Still sitting on the corner of Todd's and my bed, I picked up the telephone on the nightstand.

"Mrs. Beamer, my name is Nick Leonard from United Airlines. I'm sorry to inform you that your husband was a passenger aboard Flight 93 that has crashed in Pennsylvania."

"I know," I replied calmly. I didn't break down crying hysterically. I didn't yell or scream or make any outburst at all. The United representative sounded almost surprised that I was so calm. I didn't fully realize it then, but God was already giving me an incredible sense of peace.

The United rep gave me a telephone number where he could be reached and assured me that United would help us in every way possible. It was a number I'd call often in the days ahead.

I put down the phone and slowly nodded to the friends who had gathered around me. "That was United," I said quietly, "and they said that Todd was definitely on that plane. . . ." My voice trailed off. No more words were necessary. Brian Mumau dropped his head to his chest. Tears streamed down all our faces, but there were few emotional outbursts. Everyone in the room had already known in his or her heart of hearts that Todd was gone.

Although the United Airlines representative made no reference to terrorist activity aboard the flight, there was never a thought in my mind that this was a random accident. No one around me thought that the crash was due to an equipment failure or pilot error. Almost immediately reports circulated on the news that federal aviation authorities had reason to believe that the plane had been hijacked in a similar manner as those that had struck the World Trade Center and the Pentagon. There were even reports that some people had made cellular telephone calls from the plane before it had gone down.

Strangely, I felt some sense of relief in knowing that Todd had been aboard a plane that had crashed without hitting a building or another national landmark, causing further death and destruction or calamity in our country.

Tragic as it was, the plane had gone down in a reclaimed field that had once been a coal strip mine and was now a grassy meadow in a rural area of Pennsylvania. It was the only terrorist attack that day in which no lives were lost on the ground as a result of the crash.

In Washington, people with stunned expressions streamed into the streets as many government office buildings were evacuated. Few people panicked, though all over the city people scampered to their vehicles, trying to get home to their loved ones. They often found familiar highways blocked by authorities or clogged with traffic.

Peggy Beamer tried desperately to reach Todd's younger sister, Michele, who worked at George Washington University, not far from the Pentagon. The phone circuits in the nation's capital were jammed. Peggy was eventually able to contact Michele by means of e-mail. Meanwhile, Todd's Aunt Bonnie, a dentist, whose office is a block and a half from the White House, got a call through to Peggy.

When Peggy told her about my phone call, Bonnie said, "I'll get Michele and we'll be right out."

"I'm okay. Don't worry about me," Peggy responded valiantly.

On the way to Peggy's home, Bonnie and Michele wondered how they might inform David, Todd's dad, who was still in California conducting an important meeting for his business. They didn't want him to learn the news about Todd on television. At Peggy's house, her minister and other friends had already gathered, offering condolences and comfort, when I called a second time to confirm our fears that Todd had been on the plane.

By that time, our home in Cranbury was swarming with people as well. Rev. Bob Cushman, Todd's and my pastor, was among the first to arrive, along with Dr. Al Hickok, the professional counselor at our church. They came upstairs and prayed with me. Not knowing in what state of mind they might find me, they seemed almost surprised that I was cogent and able to function somewhat rationally.

The telephone rang constantly, and since we were hanging on for any morsel of information from United Airlines, we quickly decided it was easier to answer the calls than to let them go to the answering machine. Doug MacMillan and Brian Mumau handled the phones and logistical matters. Members of our Care Circle and others from the community and church brought in food all day long, feeding the many people who gathered at our home, cleaning up messes, running errands, and taking care of the children. Thankfully, the boys were oblivious to the horror of the day. They played with children of visitors and friends all day long, inside the house and outside. Since they were accustomed to having other people visiting in our home and enjoyed having friends over to play frequently, they probably didn't detect anything out of the ordinary—other than the inordinate number of people around.

Mom got in late Tuesday afternoon, accompanied by the pastor of her church in Peekskill. The normally 90-minute trip took close to four hours due to blocked roads and detours they negotiated to get to New Jersey. Before leaving home, Mom had called Paul and his wife, Jet, and told them the awful news. "I can't tell Jonathan over the phone," she said to Paul. "Please go to Gordon College and pick up

Jonathan, and meet us at Lisa's." Paul and Jet drove from Albany, New York, to Boston, hoping to intercept Jonathan before he heard the news from someone else. But they were too late. Just as they arrived at his dorm, someone told Jonathan that Todd had died.

My youngest brother's response was unbridled anger. He screamed and smashed his fists against the wall, venting his rage at an unseen but deeply felt enemy. Paul and Jet stayed overnight and, with Jonathan, drove to Cranbury the following day.

Meanwhile, my sister, Holly, had been driving in the Chicago area when she heard the news about Flight 93. Although she had no idea that Todd was traveling that day, she had "a bad feeling about Todd." When Mom confirmed her fears, Holly was overwhelmed, but her first reaction was to try to get to me so she could be of help. But there were no planes flying; she'd have to wait.

Most of this went on without my knowledge while I was sequestered in the bedroom, although I was cognizant that people were there in our home, taking care of the myriad details. So many people pitched in to help during those days that I'll never be able to thank them all. But God knows. Most important, friends from around the world wrapped us in their love, lifting us up in prayer.

At one point in the middle of the day, during a lull in the activity in my room, I was staring blankly into space. I looked across Todd's and my bed, and there was Jan Pittas, one of our more quiet-natured friends, just sitting on the opposite corner of the bed, quietly praying for me, not talking aloud. Not talking at all. I didn't want to talk; I wasn't able to talk, and with her sweet, gentle spirit, Jan knew better than to try to talk to me. But her presence in the room was comforting. *Thank you, God, for sending Jan,* I prayed.

In those days following the crash, this truth became even more real to me: God knows exactly *what* we need . . . *when* we need it.

Even when I tried to rest, I could hardly sleep for more than an hour, and being pregnant, I didn't want to take any medication to help me sleep. I'd break down crying sporadically and then struggle to pull myself together for a while. I'd just lie on the bed, staring into nothingness, sometimes drifting in my mind but never really falling into a deep sleep. When I couldn't sleep, I'd get out of bed and sit in our bedroom chair for hours.

The most unsettling moments came when I thought about the baby I was carrying. Todd and I had been so excited as the pregnancy progressed. Now, as my hands grazed my belly, I was reminded that I was now a single parent of two children, expecting another. I had always felt that as long as Todd was here, everything would be all right. Now he was gone, and at times the thought was overwhelming to me. "I can't do this," I sobbed quietly. "Oh, God, how am I going to raise this baby without Todd?"

■　■　■　■

In San Francisco, Rob Simons, a friend of Peggy and David's, interrupted David's meeting and conveyed an emergency message that he needed to call Peggy right away. Peggy's 92-year-old dad, Judd Jackson, had not been well, nor had David's father, so when David first heard there was an emergency, he feared it might be a problem with one of their parents. When Peggy informed Todd's father of the reason for her call, he just held on to the phone and shook. He couldn't fathom that the life of his son, his only son, had been suddenly and violently snuffed out.

David and friends Rob Simons, David Wright, and Chuck Fonner began formulating a plan to get David back home. No planes were flying because of the national security ban on air travel, imposed shortly after the attack on the World Trade Center and the Pentagon. United Airlines assured David they'd get him on a flight home as soon as the skies reopened, but nobody could guess when that might be. When David decided to drive his company car, Rob said, "If you are going to drive all the way across the country, I'm going with you."

The two men drove literally from sea to sea, all the way from San Francisco to Washington, D.C., and then on to New Jersey. "As we crossed the country, I had a chance to see again just how vast and beautiful our nation is, and how much our freedom and way of life are worth fighting for," David later observed.

It was a good reminder for all of us—and a needed one in the days ahead, as more details about United Flight 93 were revealed.

■ ■ ■ ■

Todd's longtime buddy Keith Franz, now a youth pastor in Central Pennsylvania, first heard the news of the terrorist attacks on his car radio. Racing at 85 miles per hour to get home, he found Sandy already in front of the television. They watched the unfolding scene for about two hours, never thinking that Todd could have been on board one of the planes. Keith went to church to prepare for his Tuesday-evening youth-group meeting, wondering, *How can I help the kids make sense of something so senseless as these terrorist attacks?* The youth meeting would be absorbed by a prayer vigil the church planned for that evening—similar to many others observed across America that night.

Around 1:00 P.M. Keith was at his desk preparing his notes for the evening service when Sandy called. "Keith, you have to come home right now," she said.

Keith could tell by Sandy's voice that she was shaken. He didn't even question her; he simply replied, "Okay." He dropped what he was doing and drove the five-minute stretch to their home.

When he stepped inside the house, Sandy met him in the hallway. "Flight 93 that crashed in Pennsylvania . . ."

"Yeah, I know. . . ."

"Keith, Lisa called. Todd was on that flight."

Keith staggered into the family room and slumped into a chair. He couldn't speak; he simply wept and wept.

"I think I should call Lisa," he said after a while. When he dialed my number, one of the family friends answered and told me he was on the line. Keith and I tried to talk, but the words refused to form. "It wasn't supposed to be this way . . . ," Keith said over and over as he cried on the phone.

"I know, Keith; I know," I replied.

■ ■ ■ ■

Stan Ueland, who had accompanied Todd and me on the trip to Rome, was back at work in his office on the 45th floor of the Sears Tower in Chicago when he first heard the news of the terrorist attacks. One of the largest potential targets in the Midwest, the Sears Tower was soon evacuated. Stan headed straight for home where he and his wife, Kathleen, sat glued to their television screens. Upon learning of the crash of Flight 93, Stan said to Kathleen, "With as many people as Oracle has traveling to our corporate headquarters, I've got a feeling we're going to hear that someone associated with Oracle was aboard one of those flights." When the telephone rang and Stan saw Keith Franz's name on his caller ID, he knew instantly why Keith was calling.

"Todd was on the flight, wasn't he?" Stan said before Keith even said hello.

"Yes, he was," Keith confirmed.

■ ■ ■ ■

Later that night Keith called me back. We talked for about 20 minutes, and in the course of the conversation ran the gamut from extreme sorrow to actually being able to laugh about some things that Todd had said or done. We both knew that Todd was in heaven and had no doubt we'd see him again. It felt good to laugh a little in the midst of our pain and loss. To me, and perhaps to Keith as well, being able to laugh in the face of death was therapeutic.

As it came time to prepare places for everyone to sleep

on Tuesday night, air mattresses seemed to appear out of thin air. The Care Circle thought of everything, and without fanfare or expectation of thanks, credit, or notice, they went about doing whatever needed to be done. David and Drew were delighted to have so much company in the house. They had no idea what was going on, and I was in no condition to tell them yet, but I knew I couldn't put it off much longer.

16

HOW TO TELL
THE CHILDREN?

ON WEDNESDAY MORNING, September 12—Peggy
Beamer's birthday as well as my dad's—I got up before
sunrise and prepared myself mentally and spiritually for
one of the most challenging experiences of my life—telling
my children that their father would never be coming home
again. I knew this was going to be a difficult day, and I
wanted to talk with the boys privately before things got too
hectic. Especially David. Drew was only 19 months old, so
I wasn't too worried about explaining to him. He was just
beginning to understand when I said such things as "Go to
the fridge and get your milk cup." David, however, was
three and a half and inquisitive about everything.

When Mom came downstairs, I told her what I planned
to do. I forced myself to ignore 17-year-old visions of Mom
telling my brother Paul, Holly, and me that our father had
died. It all seemed too familiar. At the same time, I drew
strength from that experience, knowing that God causes all
things to work together for good to those of us who love

him. I could already see how he was using the experience of our dad's unexpected death to help us cope with the loss of Todd. And I could already envision my family members being a resource for my children someday. In the chambers of my heart and mind, I could even imagine my brother Jonathan—who was nearly two when our dad died—someday sitting down with David and Drew and saying something such as, "I understand what it's like to lose your dad when you're so young that you never got to know him. I felt the same way when I was growing up."

Mom's voice nudged me back to the present. "Do you want me to go along with you?" she asked softly.

"No, I think I should talk to David alone." I wanted David to be focused on what I was telling him, and that would be tougher if my mom was with us.

As soon as I heard David stirring, I went into his bedroom to talk with him. He was wearing his favorite Buzz Lightyear pajamas that I'd bought him a few months earlier. The pajamas brought me up short when I saw them. The boys loved Buzz Lightyear from the Disney animated movie *Toy Story,* so when I found the pajamas, I couldn't pass them by. The day I'd purchased them, Todd had been working at home in his office while the boys were napping. I couldn't wait to show Todd my find, so I took the pajamas into his office and held them up in front of him. *"Look what I found!"* I mouthed the words silently because Todd was on a conference call with a customer.

Todd's eyes brightened, and he smiled broadly when he saw the pj's. He nodded to me and gave me a thumbs-up as if to say, *The guys are going to love these!*

Sure enough, the Buzz Lightyear pajamas were a huge hit with the boys.

Now, wearing his special pajamas, David wiped the sleep out of his eyes. I hugged David and nodded toward his large, orange basketball beanbag on the floor. "Let's sit down a minute, Big Dave. I want to talk with you." I was concerned that I communicate the awful news correctly, because I knew from my mom's counseling practice, and from our own experience following my dad's death, that kids sometimes have difficulty understanding the finality of death. It's hard for them to comprehend that the person who has died won't be coming back in this life.

We sat down together on the beanbag, and I held David close to me on my lap. I started by talking about airplanes. David had flown in airplanes before, and he understood what it meant to land and take off. We had flown together as a family to Orlando, and David remembered that trip better than most. He knew that Todd flew on planes a lot, too.

I said, "David, Daddy was flying on an airplane yesterday . . . and you know that most of the time, airplanes are safe . . . but sometimes they have accidents."

David looked at me as if to say, *Great, Mom. Why in the world are we talking about airplanes before we've even had breakfast?*

"David, the plane that Daddy was on yesterday had an accident, and . . . and it hit the ground real hard. Everyone was hurt badly . . . and died." I was struggling for a way to describe what it means to die, since David had no context in which to place the experience of death. Nobody he had ever known well in his three and a half years had died.

I tried to explain, "When a person dies, he can't come back home and he can't call us on the phone. He can't talk to us and we can't talk to him. Because Daddy loved Jesus, he went to be with God in heaven . . . and you and Drew and I will be there with Daddy someday, but today, we're not. . . ."

"But Daddy's going to be coming off the plane, right?" David asked.

"No, not this time." I gently stressed the point that Todd wouldn't be coming back. "Daddy wanted to come back, but he couldn't," I told David. "He loved us, and we love him, and we can still talk about him, but Daddy won't be coming home and we won't see him here anymore."

I was trying so hard to be calm. But all the while I was praying silently, *Oh, God! Please help me get this across to David, because I don't think I can keep going back over this again and again.* I was happy to answer any questions the boys might have, but I didn't want them to be searching for Todd, or thinking he'd be back or that they could contact him. And I didn't want to have to reiterate the whole thing.

David didn't cry; he didn't get angry; he just looked at me with love and trust. I wasn't sure if he truly understood or not until Todd's older sister, Melissa, and her husband, Greg, arrived at our house later that week from their home in Michigan. They hadn't visited since we'd moved into our new home, and David was giving them a tour of the house. When they came to Todd's and my bedroom, Greg asked, "And is this your mommy and daddy's room?"

"No," David answered. "This is just my mommy's room now, because my daddy is gone."

■ ■ ■ ■

For days following September 11, I could tell that David was trying to understand what had happened to his daddy. It was a reality that none of us wanted to accept. Occasionally David would get what he thought was a good idea. "If Daddy's plane had hit a trampoline, Mom, then nobody would have gotten hurt. It could have just bounced, bounced, and bounced back up in the air."

How's a mom supposed to respond to that?

On another day, David was playing with a toy airplane. He held the plane above the floor as though he were flying it through the room. "Mommy, when we went to Disney World, our plane landed like this." David eased his plane down to the floor. "When Daddy's plane landed, it went like this. . . ." David dropped his plane straight down to the floor. My heart dropped along with it.

Sometimes I'd overhear David talking to himself or to someone else, saying, "Most airplanes are safe, but Daddy's wasn't safe."

Since then we've had many conversations clarifying what dying means, and David has had many questions, some of which have nearly knocked the breath out of me at times. But one thing has utterly amazed me: David has never questioned the finality of Todd's death in this lifetime. One of his questions that was the most difficult to answer was why, if Daddy loved us so much, would he want to go and live with Jesus?

I tried to explain to him that, if given a choice that day, Daddy would have preferred to come home. "Where he is right now is a great place, but if he could, he'd want to be with us at home," I told David. "Daddy wanted to go to heaven someday because he knew that being together with God there would be better than anything that we can imagine here. But he wanted to finish being your daddy first, and it makes him sad that he couldn't finish that job."

"What happens when Daddy is sad now?" David asked.

"Well, it says in the Bible that in heaven God comes and wipes away all our tears. And he reminds Daddy that he will see all of us again, and we'll all be in heaven together. That helps Daddy to be very happy."

We talked about how a person gets to make some important choices in life. "When a person dies, those who love God choose to go to where God is; those who don't love God choose to go to where God isn't, and that place is very sad because there is no love there," I tried to explain delicately.

David seemed to consider my words. Then he looked back at me with all the innocence of childhood and answered, "Mommy, when I die, I'm gonna choose to come *home.*"

17

A PHONE CALL
FROM HEAVEN

FROM WEDNESDAY, September 12, to Friday, September 14, our home was filled with people nearly 24 hours a day. It was such a strange time, since in addition to the normal mourning that a family goes through at the loss of a loved one, the entire nation was also in mourning as a result of the events of September 11. Many of the people in mourning were also angry, resolute, and ready to respond in whatever way our nation's leaders deemed appropriate.

I never turned on the television during those days, but others in our home wanted to keep abreast of the newscasts. Death tolls from the World Trade Center and the Pentagon attacks were updated and revised almost hourly, as nobody seemed to know for sure just how many lives were lost at those locations. The number of people who died in the crash of Flight 93 was confirmed at 37 passengers—four of whom were terrorists—plus the pilot, copilot, and five flight attendants.

■　■　■　■

Usually I am totally in charge of what goes on in our home.
But in the days following September 11, our friends took
over and did it all—including cooking, cleaning, and
arranging housing for anyone who needed it. Each morning
I came downstairs while it was still dark and tried to
straighten things up a bit around the house. I'd put dishes
away and also stash all the things I didn't recognize as
belonging to our family in a closet that I designated as the
"lost and found" area.

My personality type requires some alone time, almost
an impossibility around our house during that week. So for
me the quiet moments alone in the morning, putting our
house back together in some orderly fashion, gave me a
sense of normalcy in a very abnormal time.

Mom worried that I was trying to do too much. "You
don't need to be housecleaning," she said. "We have lots of
other people who can do those things."

"Don't worry, Mom," I told her. "I *need* to be doing
something. If you ever see me just sitting around when my
home is in disarray, *then* you can worry. Because then you'll
know I've lost my mind. As long as you see me trying to
keep things organized and orderly, you'll know I'm okay!"

Todd's mom, his Aunt Bonnie, and his younger sister,
Michele, arrived on Wednesday, as did Keith Franz. Along
with Pastor Cushman, Elaine Mumau, and a few other
friends, we began to plan a special memorial service for
Todd to be held on Sunday afternoon at three o'clock. Hopefully the airlines would be flying by then, or at least those

who wanted to attend would have time to drive in for the service. We gathered some mementos and photographs to display and to use in a video presentation during the memorial service, and we selected some songs and Bible passages that were especially meaningful to Todd and to me.

Unlike the families of victims at the World Trade Center or the Pentagon, we had no hope of finding anyone alive in the wreckage. By all accounts, the plane had virtually disintegrated in the fiery crash. United Airlines clearly implied that there would be few, if any, remains to bury, and any personal effects found at the crash site might not be forthcoming for months. Consequently, I thought it was important to have a ceremony as soon as possible that would allow everyone to acknowledge Todd's death. Usually when a family member passes away, a funeral service is held within three or four days. Since we wouldn't be having a viewing, and most family members and friends were either with us or on their way, it only made sense to do the memorial service soon.

By now the family had heard that other passengers aboard Flight 93 had contacted loved ones by cell phone and that the passengers had planned some sort of attempt to overthrow the hijackers. Everyone speculated about Todd's possible involvement.

One question nagged at me: If others were making calls aboard the flight, why hadn't Todd called? He lived with a cell phone practically attached to his ear. We could only imagine what it must have been like during the final minutes of that doomed flight. But if others found the means and the time to call, why hadn't Todd?

In my lower moments, I even thought that perhaps Todd had been murdered by the terrorists. I didn't dare allow myself to dwell on such morbid thoughts, but that might have explained why he didn't call anyone.

I overheard several guys at the house as they discussed what might have happened as passengers tried to take back the plane. "I know Todd was right in the middle of them, leading the charge," one fellow said. I smiled slightly at our friend's comment. It was sheer conjecture; we had no tangible reason to believe that Todd had done anything to fight back against the hijackers. Yet, knowing Todd's personality and character, it seemed logical to assume that if anyone aboard the plane made any attempt to foil the terrorists' efforts, Todd would have been involved somehow. That's just the kind of person he was.

Interestingly, unknown to me at the time, Larry Ellison, the energetic leader of the Oracle Corporation, sent out an e-mail to all of the company's employees on Thursday, September 13. In a moving letter, Larry informed the company that a number of Oracle employees were involved in the tragedy of September 11, and at least seven employees were still missing in the World Trade Center rubble. Larry also told the company that Todd had died in the crash of Flight 93.

Then, to the amazement of many, Larry continued to eulogize Todd in an almost prophetic manner. "We know Todd Beamer is dead," Larry reported. "We believe he died when he and other passengers aboard Flight 93 tried to recover the hijacked airplane from the terrorists. . . . Todd's courageous actions may not have saved the lives of his fellow passengers, but he helped prevent the airplane from reaching its target—our nation's Capitol. Considering the devastation wrought by the other aircraft, it is unquestionable that Todd's brave actions, and [those] of his fellow passengers, saved countless lives on the ground."

Clearly Larry was convinced that Todd had been involved. How did Larry know that? The FBI hadn't made any announcement to that effect. Todd's name had not shown up in any reports indicating that he might have been involved in some way. Yet Larry, like many of us, couldn't imagine Todd Beamer sitting idly by while terrorists threatened to hurt others.

Friday evening, around nine o'clock, the house was once again filled with friends and relatives when I received a call from Nick Leonard, our family liaison with United Airlines. "Lisa, I have some information for you," Nick said. "But you might want to go to a quiet place before I tell you."

Nick was the man who had first informed me that Todd was on Flight 93. What could he possibly tell me that would be any worse than that? "And you might want to take someone along with you," Nick added.

I thought, *Okay, what in the world is this guy going to tell me?*

Nevertheless, I motioned to my brother Paul, and we went upstairs to my bedroom and took Nick's call there. Slowly and carefully, Nick began to give me the news. I could tell he wasn't sure how I was going to take it.

"Lisa, the FBI has released information that Todd *did* make a phone call from the flight. He called on the GTE

Airfone aboard the plane, and the call went to an operator in the Chicago area. The FBI has been keeping the information private until they've had an opportunity to review the material. But now they've released it."

As Nick was speaking to me, I was relaying the information to Paul. Nick went on. "I have a written summary of the call, and I'm not sure what you want me to do with it."

"Do you have it in front of you?"

"Yes, I do."

"Well, read it to me!" I said straightforwardly.

Nick read a summary written by a GTE supervisor, Lisa Jefferson, who had taken over the call when it came through one of her operators' switchboard stations. It was clear from the information Nick read that Todd hadn't been murdered by the terrorists. Quite the contrary—he had been actively involved in communicating with someone on the ground, providing information about the hijackers in hopes that somehow he and some of the other passengers could devise a plan to thwart the terrorists' efforts.

As Nick relayed the operator's summary, I scrawled quickly in staccato form:

> Is there a recording of the call? No, she would have had to leave her station to record a call, and feared being cut off. A miracle that his call stayed connected b/c volume of calls
> Do we know where he was sitting?
> 10 in front

27 in back

Flight attendant next to him—told him what had happened in first class

What do they want? Ransom?

Todd—Jeremy Glick discussed together to "jump" [hijacker]

Said, going down, we're ok, we're coming back up, we're turning around—I think we're headed north

Completed Lord's Prayer with him

Asked Jesus to help him—knew he wasn't going to make it—

Told about family, made a promise to call me to tell that he loved us very much

Todd said, are you ready, let's roll—put phone down but never came back on

Could hear screaming in background

Feels like she made a fine friend.

By the time Nick finished telling me the content of Todd's call, I was in tears. The information confirmed to me that Todd was "who he was" right to the very end of his life. It was a tremendous comfort to know that in his last moments, his faith in God remained strong, and his love for us, his family, was at the forefront of his thoughts. I was glad to know that Todd felt he had some control of his destiny, that he might be able to effect change even to the end. The words "Let's roll!" were especially significant to me. Just hearing that made me smile, partially because it was "so Todd," but also because it showed he felt he could still do something positive in the midst of a crisis situation.

Of course his final "I love you" will live with me forever.

"If you'd like to talk with the operator, she said it would be okay to call her," Nick told me.

"Yes, I would love to talk with her." Nick gave me the telephone number where I could reach Lisa Jefferson, the last person known to have spoken with my husband. Did I want to talk with her? Absolutely!

Paul and I went downstairs and called everyone together. Through our tears, we recounted the message Nick Leonard had passed on to us. The change in the mood of the family and friends was almost palpable. We were still grieving, and although the information could never change the horrible sense of loss we felt, we were given a bit of joy in knowing that Todd hadn't died a helpless victim and might even, in fact, have prevented others from becoming victims.

Somewhere Larry Ellison must have been smiling.

It was such good news that we had to share it. I called Todd's mom, who had returned to Washington to await the return of David, Todd's dad, who was still driving across the nation. We were able to contact David by cell phone as he made the cross-country journey. For all of us, even more significant and encouraging than Todd's heroic actions aboard Flight 93 was the knowledge that his faith—and ours—could withstand the ultimate test.

On Saturday morning I called the GTE Airfone supervisor, Lisa Jefferson, and for the first time learned what Todd had said and done, and what had truly happened aboard Flight 93.

18

RELIVING THE
TAKEOVER

AS THE WORLD awaited the reopening of American
airspace after the 9-11 tragedies, Nick Leonard, our helpful
United Airlines family liaison, had my sister, Holly
Brosious, booked on one flight after another, only to have
them canceled. Finally she arrived on Friday night, just in
time to hear the good news about Todd's phone call.

That same night, as further encouragement, my brother
Paul and his wife, Jet, informed the family that they were
expecting a baby. We were all excited at the news, and I
was especially glad to know the baby I was carrying would
have a family member around the same age.[5] Perhaps even
more significant, although none of us verbalized it at the
time, was the reminder that life does go on. In the midst of
tragic loss, God was bringing a new set of miracles into
being.

Early Saturday morning our friend Doug MacMillan

[5]Paul and Jet's baby, Emmalyn Kathleen Brosious, was born on April 17, 2002,
so Morgan, our daughter, does have a cousin her own age!

accompanied me into Todd's home office to call Lisa Jefferson. As I had done the night before with Nick and Paul, I wanted to relay information to Doug as I received it from Lisa so we would be better able to remember it. Nervously I dialed her phone number.

Although I was anxious to speak with her, I wasn't expecting the overwhelming emotion I felt during our conversation. I was much more emotional talking to Lisa Jefferson than I had been with Nick Leonard the night before. I think it was because she was the last human link with Todd, and I knew I'd never be able to talk with him again. Nick could read the words off the page, but Lisa could provide a firsthand account of what Todd had said and done. She could tell me of Todd's demeanor, the sound and inflection of his voice, and the faith that surged through him during those last moments.

I was already crying before Lisa picked up the telephone. "This is Lisa Beamer," I sobbed, trying in vain to maintain my composure. Lisa didn't seem to mind. She just waited patiently until I was ready.

First she asked me some questions based on information she'd learned from Todd, letting me know that it was truly Todd she had spoken to on the phone. "Do you have two boys whose names are David and Andrew?" she asked.

"Yes, I do."

"Are you expecting a baby?"

"Yes, I am, in January. Todd told you all of that?" I asked.

"Yes, he did," Lisa replied.

As we talked further, I quickly discovered that Lisa was quiet and soft-spoken but extremely factual and articulate. I could understand easily why Todd would have related to her and trusted her help in the critical circumstances he faced. She was a strong woman, yet she also seemed to be an extremely caring and compassionate person.

■ ■ ■ ■

With the information Lisa Jefferson provided and the subsequent reports that have become known to me, I have been able to reconstruct what Todd experienced the morning of September 11.

I can picture him boarding the plane and settling in to his seat in row 10 for the six-hour flight from Newark to San Francisco. I have no doubt that when Todd entered the aircraft, one of the first things he did was unpack his laptop and pull out some work. From cell-phone records we know that he spoke to Jonathan Oomrigar at Oracle about their meeting later that day. He also left some other voice-mail messages for business associates.

The plane was scheduled to take off at 8:00 A.M., and in fact the Boeing 757 did push back from Gate A-17 at 8:01. But, as is often the case at Newark International, runway traffic delayed the takeoff. For the next 40 minutes the plane remained on the ground.

Meanwhile, in Boston, American Flight 11 took off from Logan Airport at 8:00 sharp; United Flight 175 followed close behind. Both Boston planes were scheduled to fly to Los Angeles that morning. In Washington, D.C., American

Flight 77, also headed to Los Angeles, took off from Dulles Airport at 8:10 A.M. Of the four fuel-laden cross-country flights with terrorists aboard, only one remained on the ground: Flight 93.

Most of us get frustrated in traffic jams at times, especially when our plans are disrupted. But the traffic jam in which Flight 93 sat that morning may have been a key factor in saving thousands of lives—and perhaps even our nation's Capitol.

As irritating as the delay might have been to others, Todd probably took it in stride and viewed the traffic jam as an opportunity to get a little more work done—a bit of time to make one last cell-phone call before the flight attendants asked that electronic devices be put away until the plane was airborne.

The plane carried a relatively light load that morning— seven crew members, including Captain Jason Dahl, First Officer LeRoy Homer, and five flight attendants; and 37 passengers, mostly men and women on business, a few couples on vacation, and several students heading back to school. While for most of the passengers it was a routine flight, some of the less experienced travelers may have been a bit nervous about airline safety at takeoff. Yet no one knew that four male passengers in their twenties planned to die on that plane.

The four Middle Eastern–looking young men, all deeply religious, were led by Ziad Samir Jarrah, who sat in first-class seat 1B, the seat closest to the cockpit door. The 27-year-old Lebanese man was a licensed pilot who had taken flying lessons as well as self-defense classes in Florida less than a year earlier. Jarrah's cohorts were in seats 3C, 3D, and 6B.

At least one of the young religious zealots carried a copy of specific handwritten instructions from Mohamed Atta, the Egyptian ringleader of the four groups of Islamic terrorists assigned to U.S. planes that day. Atta's five pages of instructions (later found at the crash site) included spiritual readings the terrorists were to meditate on the night before the attacks, as well as practical matters such as "bathe carefully, shave excess body hair," and "make sure you are clean, your clothes are clean, including your shoes." Possibly these instructions were for spiritual purification or possibly to avoid notice. Most telling were Atta's pointed reminders to bring "knives, your will, your IDs, your passport, all your papers."

The terrorists were told to clench their teeth when the moment to strike came. They were to "shout, *Allahu akbar* [Arabic for "God is great"] because this strikes fear in the hearts of the unbelievers. . . . When the confrontation begins, strike like champions who do not want to go back to this world."

The directions were clearly intended for young men going on a mission from which they would not return. Especially perplexing and somewhat frightening are the deluded references to God—not the God of the Bible but a god who would endorse murder and hate, a god clearly created in the minds of these men to justify their own evil intentions. Laced throughout the suicide-mission notes are exhortations such as, "Obey God, his messenger, and don't fight among [yourselves] when you become weak.

And stand fast; God will stand with those who stood
fast.

"You should pray; you should fast. You should ask God
for guidance; you should ask God for help. . . . Continue to
pray throughout this night. . . . Purify your heart and clean
it from all earthly matters. The time of fun and waste has
gone. The time of judgment has arrived. Hence we need to
utilize those few hours to ask God for forgiveness."

Atta's instructions included several promises of eternal
life to the terrorists. "You will be entering paradise. You
will be entering the happiest life, everlasting life."

In the last page of the instructions, headed "When you
enter the plane," the hijackers were given special prayers
to say. "Oh, God, open all doors for me. Oh, God, who
answers prayers and answers those who ask you, I am
asking you for your help. I am asking you for forgiveness.
I am asking you to lighten my way. I am asking you to lift
the burden I feel. Oh, God, you who open all doors, please
open all doors for me. . . ."

The document closes with the statement "God, I trust in
you. God, I lay myself in your hands. There is no God but
God. . . . We are of God, and to God we return."

■ ■ ■ ■

Following the delay—I can't help but wonder what might
have happened had it been a few minutes longer—United
Flight 93 took off from Newark International Airport, across
the river from New York City, at 8:42 A.M. The plane was
still climbing over the New York–New Jersey coastline

when, just six minutes later, American Airlines Flight 11 blasted into the north tower of the World Trade Center. The skies were clear on the morning of September 11, an absolutely gorgeous day in New York, and one of the men in the cockpit of Todd's plane noticed the smoke rising from below. "Is everything okay on the ground?" he asked air-traffic control.

"Everything is fine," he was told.

Flight 93 continued climbing to its cruising altitude and headed west, across New Jersey into Pennsylvania. At 9:03 A.M., United Flight 175 smashed into the south tower of the World Trade Center. With both buildings burning in New York, United Airlines flashed an alert to all its cockpit computer screens: "Beware cockpit intrusion." From high above Harrisburg, Pennsylvania, not far from where my parents grew up and where Keith Franz now lived, Flight 93 responded, "Confirmed."

Ironically, activities in the cabin were quite normal, as flight attendants served breakfast and passengers relaxed or worked. Around 9:25, one of the pilots checked in with Cleveland's air-traffic control center, which normally takes over guidance of flights as they move across the Midwest. "Good morning!" one of the pilots said sprightly from the Flight 93 cockpit. By now the pilots had learned that something was awry in New York, and they calmly asked Cleveland for more information.

About that time Cleveland controllers were receiving bomb threats on the ground, as were controllers in Boston—possibly in an attempt to create further fear and chaos and to distract controllers from tracking the hijacked planes. A minute later, at 9:28, the Cleveland controllers clearly heard screams over the open mike aboard Flight 93.

In Sarasota, Florida, President Bush was reading to a class of schoolchildren when he was interrupted and told of an "apparent terrorist attack." Aboard Flight 93 and the three other doomed planes, the attack wasn't apparent; it was deadly.

The controllers radioed the plane, but there was no answer. After about 40 seconds, the Cleveland controllers heard more muffled cries. "Get out of here!" an English-speaking voice implored. "Get out of here!" Whether the crew member was frantically yelling at the hijackers or warning someone else who may have attempted to offer assistance is unclear. What *is* certain, however, is that the captain and copilot were yanked out of the cockpit. Passengers, including Todd, later reported seeing two people lying motionless on the floor near the cockpit, possibly with their throats cut.

No one is certain how the terrorists got into the cockpit. Some speculate that they preyed on an older flight attendant, threatening to slit her throat if the pilots didn't come out of the cockpit. Or they may simply have broken through the thin door that separated the cockpit from the cabin. Perhaps they waited for an open door, then barged into the tight cockpit, slitting the throats of the pilots while they were still strapped in their seats. On the cockpit voice recorder there were sounds of someone choking.

As soon as the hijackers took over the plane's controls, they disengaged the autopilot. The plane bounced up and down, and Arabic voices could be heard reassuring each other, "Everything is fine." Apparently the hijackers didn't realize that the microphone was still open and their words were audible to other aircraft as well as to controllers on the ground.

Then controllers in Cleveland heard one of the hijackers, out of breath from the struggle or possibly from lugging the captain and copilot out of the way. The heavily accented voice, most likely that of Jarrah, said, "Ladies and gentlemen, it's the captain. Please sit down."

Most genuine captains of American jetliners have a fairly good grasp of English grammar. This man did not, but his ominous message stunned the passengers nonetheless. "Keep remaining sitting," he said. "We have a bomb aboard."

People in the control tower and in other planes nearby heard the hijackers telling the passengers aboard Flight 93 to remain seated, although within the next few minutes the flight attendants and passengers in the main cabin, including Todd, were herded to the back of the plane to rows 30 to 34, near the galley.

The heavily accented voice came over the air again. "This is the captain. Remain sitting. There is a bomb aboard. We are going back to the airport to have our demands. Remain quiet."

About that time the voice recorder reveals that the hijackers must have realized their mistake. They shut off the open microphone, assuming they had shut down the flow of information to the ground. But back in the cabin, the communication airwaves were crackling. . . .

19

PLOTS ABOARD
FLIGHT 93

THE FIRST KNOWN phone call came from Tom Burnett of
San Ramon, California, a father of three little girls and an
executive for Thoretec, a health-care company. A big man
who had quarterbacked his high school football team, Tom
was seated in the first-class cabin next to Mark Bingham, a
San Francisco publicist who was on his way home. Mark
had overslept that morning and had run down the A-17
gangway just as the flight attendants were about to close
the plane's door. Had he been a few minutes later, he
would have missed the flight.

Tom Burnett called his wife, Deena, at their home. A
former flight attendant herself, she immediately picked up
on the fact that something was wrong. "Are you okay?"

"No," Tom replied. "I am on the airplane, United Flight
93, and it has been hijacked." He spoke quickly and quietly.
"They've knifed a guy and there's a bomb on board. Please
call the authorities, Deena." And he hung up.

■ ■ ■ ■

Lisa Jefferson was at work at the GTE Airfone Customer Care Center in Oakbrook, Illinois, a Chicago suburb, when she first heard news of the terrorist attacks in New York and Washington, D.C. A supervisor with more than 18 years of experience at her job, she came out of her office to get more information. Just then, at about 8:45 A.M. CDT (9:45 EDT), the operator at Station 15 received an urgent call. The operator signaled for Lisa's assistance.

"She told me she had a real hijacking situation on her line," Lisa says. "I asked her what airline and the flight number. She told me it was United Flight 93. She appeared to be traumatized, so I told her I would take over.

"When I took over the call, there was a gentleman on the phone. He was very calm and soft-spoken. I introduced myself to him as Mrs. Jefferson and told him, 'I understand this plane is being hijacked. Can you please give me detailed information as to what is going on?' " Then Lisa began going through her GTE Distress-Call Manual, asking questions such as, "How many people are on board? How many hijackers? Are they armed? Are there any children on board?"

The man answered Lisa Jefferson in an equally calm manner. He was sitting next to a flight attendant who helped him relay the information: 27 passengers in coach, 10 in first class, five flight attendants, and no children that he could see. "He told me that three people had taken over the plane," said Lisa, "two with knives and one with a bomb strapped around his waist with a red belt. The two with knives had locked themselves in the cockpit. They ordered everyone to sit down, as the flight attendants were still standing. One of the flight attendants just happened to sit next to Todd in the back of the plane. The hijacker with the bomb pulled the curtain that divided first class from coach so the passengers in the back couldn't see what was going on."

But Todd did see two people on the floor. "He couldn't tell if they were dead or alive," said Lisa. "The flight attendant told him she was pretty sure it was the pilot and the copilot.

"I asked the caller's name and he told me, 'Todd Beamer.' He told me he was from Cranbury, New Jersey.

"At first I thought Todd was whispering or keeping his voice down low to prevent detection, so I told him that if at any point he thought his life might be in jeopardy for being on the line with me to put the phone down but try not to hang up—to keep the line open so I could at least hear what was going on.

"But he didn't seem to be concerned. He said he was fine. At first he said, 'Maybe I should try to call my wife.' Then he said, 'No, I just want to let someone know this is happening.' He thought the terrorists were going back to the airport and the plane would land safely."

Lisa Jefferson later told me, "He didn't want to call you and give you bad news if he didn't have to. I offered to try and connect him with you. He went back and forth on it several times before he decided against it."

I'm so glad he didn't. Had I learned about Todd's circumstances by hearing his voice from the plane, I no doubt would have lost it. I have tremendous respect for those family members and friends who received calls from hijacked flights that day and were able to maintain their composure. But I honestly don't think I would have responded so well. And Todd knew that. Todd was a smart guy. He knew I was home by myself with the boys and would have been powerless to help; moreover, he may have been concerned about our unborn baby had I gotten too upset. So I wasn't surprised to learn from Lisa that he had considered calling me and had chosen against it. Nor was I offended or hurt. In the only way he could, Todd was still looking out for me, protecting me, even in such awful circumstances.

At first, most likely, Todd thought that this hijacking would end similarly to other hijackings in our history, with the hijackers making demands, landing the plane in some location amenable to their cause, and negotiators hopefully being able to find a solution. While he recognized the danger, he didn't seem desperate.

"Todd was calm all the way through our conversation," Lisa told me. "He asked me, 'Do you know what they want? Do they want money, or ransom, or what?'

" 'I really don't know,' I told him. I didn't have a clue what they wanted. I didn't tell him about the other hijackings at that point, and I don't think he was aware of them yet. I didn't want him to get upset or excited or lose control, and I still felt that he had hope."

By now the FBI was on another line, listening in, since part of GTE's distress procedure is to notify them.

"Suddenly Todd's voice inflection went up a little bit

and he said, 'We are going down! We're going down. No, wait. We are coming back up. No, we are turning around, we are going north. . . . I really don't know where we are going. Oh, Jesus, please help us!' "

Just about 10 minutes earlier, at 9:36 A.M. EDT, the air-traffic controllers on the ground had watched their radar screens in horror as the plane made a hairpin left turn just above Cleveland, veering sharply off course and turning south at first, then east. Where was this plane going?

What actually happened in the next several minutes is unclear. Apparently the plane's autopilot and transponder—the device that emits a signal by which radar can track a plane—were switched off, and the hijackers were flying erratically. The plane began plunging, lurching, and bobbing from the altitude it had maintained previously. Perhaps the hijackers were simply trying to keep the passengers off guard by jolting them around. Todd had always talked about "flying below the radar"; now, with the transponder turned off, he actually was.

Tom Burnett called Deena a second time. "They're in the cockpit now!" he told her. He asked Deena about the World Trade Center. "Were the planes that hit it commercial passenger airliners?"

"I don't know," Deena replied.

"We're turning back to New York," he told her. "No, we're heading south." Tom said he had to go and hung up again.

Three minutes later the Pentagon was hit. The FAA ordered all airports in the country closed immediately and all airborne planes to the ground, but Flight 93 maintained its new course, heading southeast . . . straight toward Washington, D.C.

Seated somewhere near Todd was Jeremy Glick, a new father from Hewitt, New Jersey, an hour and a half from where Todd and I lived. A strong, athletic-looking guy at six feet, one inch, and 220 pounds, Jeremy was a former NCAA judo champion with a love for waterskiing. Just the type of guy with whom Todd would have struck up an instant friendship under different circumstances. As it was, the two men quickly found some common ground. Todd specifically mentioned Jeremy's name to Lisa Jefferson.

Jeremy had planned to fly out to San Francisco for a business meeting the day before, but because of the fire at the airport, his flight had been rerouted to Kennedy International. Jeremy chose instead to return home and take Tuesday's early flight out of Newark—United Flight 93.

Since Jeremy had planned to be gone, his wife, Lyz, had taken their three-month-old baby, Emmy, to visit Lyz's parents in Windham, upstate New York. Jeremy had called Lyz around 7:30 that morning before boarding, just to say a quick hello. Lyz's dad had picked up the phone and told Jeremy that Emmy had been fussing the night before, so Lyz was still sleeping. They decided to let her sleep.

"Have a good trip," Lyz's dad told Jeremy.

Now Jeremy was calling back, this time from somewhere above Cleveland. "Three Iranian-looking men wearing red headbands, one with a red box strapped to his waist, say they have a bomb and have taken control of the plane," he told Lyz.

When Lyz heard Jeremy mention a bomb, she panicked. Jeremy calmed her down, and the couple stayed on the phone for nearly 20 minutes. They told each other, "I love you," over and over.

Jeremy must have sensed the situation wasn't going to turn out well. He told Lyz he wanted her and Emmy to be happy, and that he'd respect any decisions she made in the future.

Then Jeremy said, "Lyz, I need to know something. One of the other passengers talked to his wife and said that planes had crashed into the World Trade Center. Is that true?"

Lyz was afraid to tell Jeremy what she was seeing with her own eyes. Standing in the living room, watching the television, she could see the smoke from the World Trade Center that had just collapsed. She hesitated for a moment and then said, "Please be strong, but yes, they are doing that."

"Is that where we're going, too?" Jeremy asked. Lyz told him she didn't think there was anything left of the World Trade Center.

When Tom Burnett called Deena a third time, she told him, "Tom, they just hit the Pentagon. They seem to be taking planes and driving them into landmarks all over the East Coast."

Tom told Deena he was suspicious about the hijackers' bomb. "I think they're bluffing," he told his wife. "We're going to do something. I've got to go."

About that same time, Jeremy Glick told Lyz that some of the guys in the back of the plane were talking about rushing the hijackers.

Meanwhile, other people aboard Flight 93 were calling friends and loved ones as well. Earlier that morning, Lauren Grandcolas had been delighted to learn that she could get a standby seat aboard Flight 93; it would get her home earlier than expected. She'd called and left a message for her husband to that effect. Now she called again and left another message. "We are having a little problem on the plane, but I am fine and comfortable . . . for now."

Joseph DeLuca called his dad. His girlfriend, Linda Gronlund, called her sister, telling her the combination to her safe-deposit box and how much she loved her. Marion Britton borrowed a phone to call a friend, telling him that she was sure she was going to die. She said, "They already slit two people's throats."

Mark Bingham, at six feet, five inches, was a former rugby player on a national championship team. He had once faced down an armed mugger on the streets of San Francisco. A gutsy guy and a risk taker, he had run with the bulls in Pamplona a few months previously. But when Mark called his mom, Alice Hoglan, from the plane, he seemed distracted and rattled. "Mom, this is Mark Bingham," he said. "I just want to tell you that I love you in case I don't see you again." Mark's mom heard somber voices in the background during the call, possibly laying the initial plans for a counterattack.

Flight attendant Sandy Bradshaw called her husband, a USAirways pilot, from the coach-class galley. "We've been hijacked," she told him. She also said she and some other flight attendants were filling coffeepots with boiling water to throw at the hijackers.

More than two dozen phone calls were placed from the plane that morning. Why had the hijackers permitted such easy access with the outside world? Some people have speculated that the terrorists actually wanted passengers to call, to increase the fright they felt they were inflicting and to create even more widespread havoc. Possibly they overestimated their control of the situation, or perhaps they underestimated the Americans on board, considering them too weak and timorous to fight back. For whatever reason, the terrorists made no effort to thwart the outgoing phone calls. None of the people who connected with family or friends on the ground gave any indication that they feared being caught, punished, or killed if seen making an attempt to communicate with the outside world.

It's not known whether the passengers aboard Flight 93 truly knew what a formidable force they represented that morning, and how good their chances of landing the plane safely might have been if—and what a large *if* it was—they could regain control of the cockpit.

Besides the assortment of athletic colleagues such as Jeremy Glick, Tom Burnett, and Mark Bingham, several other passengers were well able to take care of themselves. CeeCee Ross-Lyles, one of the flight attendants, was a former police officer. Lou Nacke was a human fireplug at five feet, three inches, and 200 pounds. A company manager for K·B Toys and a weight lifter, Lou had a Superman tattoo on his shoulder. When he was a little boy, he once attempted to crash through a glass window while wearing his Superman cape.

Rich Guadagno was an enforcement officer with California Fish and Wildlife and had been trained in hand-to-hand combat. Linda Gronlund, a lawyer, had a brown belt in karate. Although he was 60 years of age, William Cashman was a former paratrooper with 101st Airborne, and he was still in good shape. Alan Beaven, over six feet tall, was a former Scotland Yard prosecutor who enjoyed rock climbing as a pastime. He had a sign on his desk: "Fear—who cares?"

And then there was Todd—strong, athletic, a gamer, the go-to guy.

In addition to sheer strength, the small number of passengers had a surprising amount of aeronautical acumen. Don Greene had flown single-engine planes before he was old enough to vote. He was the vice president of Safe Flight Instrument Group, a company that made safety devices for airlines, and with some coaching from air-traffic controllers on the ground, probably could have landed the United jet. Andrew Garcia was an air-traffic controller for the Air National Guard. Working together, they could probably have brought the plane down safely . . . if . . .

20

A TEAM UNITED . . . IN LIFE AND DEATH

JEREMY GLICK was still talking with his wife, Lyz, as the counterattack plan began to be formulated among those on United Flight 93. Jeremy told Lyz that the passengers were discussing what to do, that they were going to take a vote. "What do you think we should do?" he asked his wife.

"Go for it," Lyz told him. She knew he really had no choice. It had become increasingly clear that this was not the kind of hijacking from which people escaped without injury. The terrorists weren't going to land the plane and walk away peacefully. Somebody was likely to die. And maybe a lot of people.

Unlike the passengers aboard the other hijacked flights on September 11, the passengers aboard Flight 93 had been given an unlikely gift: the inconvenience and delay caused by the traffic jam on Newark's runways, which had provided them with both time and information. The passengers dared not sit back idly while the plane streaked toward another national landmark. Better to make some attempt to recapture the cockpit.

Jeremy told Lyz that some of the passengers were debating about what they could use for weapons. He laughed nervously. "I've got my butter knife from breakfast."

*   *   *   *

About that same time, Tom Burnett called Deena, his wife, again. "We're going to do something," he told her.

A veteran flight attendant, Deena knew that resistance was not the prescribed method for dealing with hijackings. Everything in the book said, "Don't confront. Don't make waves. Just get the plane on the ground and let the authorities handle it." Understandably, she emphasized that procedure to her husband. "Tom, sit down. Please! Be still. Be quiet. Don't draw attention to yourself. Wait for the authorities."

"We can't wait, Deena," Tom replied straightforwardly. "If they are going to run this plane into the ground, we're going to do something."

"I love you, Tom. What else should I do?"

"Just pray, Deena, pray." And then Tom hung up the phone for the final time.

*   *   *   *

In the cockpit, one of the hijackers can be heard on the voice recorder telling another terrorist to "let the guys in now." Presumably the two other hijackers—the role of the fourth has never been ascertained—sensed that the passengers were becoming more difficult to control and retreated to the cockpit area.

One of the hijackers in the cockpit began to pray. Then the hijackers discussed using an ax, whose sole purpose was to break the glass around the fire extinguisher in case of fire in the cockpit, to subdue the passengers. Instead they turned off the autopilot and rocked the jet, probably in an attempt to send any would-be attackers reeling.

■　■　■　■

Lisa Jefferson indicated to me that at several points during their 15-minute phone call, Todd put the phone down, moved around the plane to talk with other passengers, and then returned to their conversation. Lisa told me, "If I hadn't known it was a real hijacking, I'd have thought it was a crank call, because Todd was so rational and methodical about what he was doing."

She told me of Todd's involvement in the counterattack and the message that Todd had asked her to convey to me. She recalled, "Todd asked me, 'In case I don't make it through this, would you please call my family and let them know how much I love them?' I promised him that I would.

"He told me that he had two boys, David and Andrew, and said his wife was also expecting another baby in January.

"After that the plane took another dive down and began flying erratically. There was another outburst, and I could tell in Todd's voice that he was feeling nervous but still calm. When the plane jolted, Todd shouted, 'Oh, God!'

"Then he said, 'Lisa!' I had not given him my name, as I had introduced myself as Mrs. Jefferson.

"And I said, 'Yes?'

"He said, 'Oh, that's my wife's name.'

"And I said, 'That's my name too, Todd.'

"Then he asked me if he didn't make it, would I keep that promise, and find his wife and children and let them know he loved his family very much. He even gave me his home phone number. When the plane was flying in an erratic fashion, he thought he had lost connection with me. He was hollering, 'Lisa! Lisa!'

"I said, 'I am still here; I am not going anywhere. I will be here as long as you will.'

"He seemed concerned about losing the connection and just wanted me to stay on the phone. I told him, 'I'm not going anywhere. I'm going to be right here with you.'

" 'We're going to do something. . . . I don't think we're going to get out of this thing,' Todd said. 'I'm going to have to go out on faith.' He told me they were talking about jumping the guy with the bomb."

"Are you sure that's what you want to do, Todd?" Lisa asked.

"It's what we have to do," Todd told her.

"He asked me to recite the Lord's Prayer with him," Lisa said, "and I did. We recited it together from the start to the finish:

> *Our Father which art in heaven,*
> *Hallowed be thy name.*
> *Thy kingdom come.*
> *Thy will be done in earth, as it is in heaven.*
> *Give us this day our daily bread.*

And forgive us our trespasses,
as we forgive those who trespass against us.
And lead us not into temptation,
but deliver us from evil:
For thine is the kingdom, and the power,
and the glory, for ever. Amen.[6]

At the conclusion of the prayer aboard Flight 93, Todd said, "Jesus, help me."

"I knew that if Todd didn't make it," Lisa told me, "he was definitely going to the right place."

Although I'd never before heard of Todd reciting the Lord's Prayer in pressure situations, I wasn't surprised to hear he had quoted it. Recently our pastor had taught a 12-week series of lessons on the Lord's Prayer. Todd had known the prayer since childhood, but each line of it had become more special to him as he discovered how fraught with meaning it really was. At the close of the series, the pastor passed out Lord's Prayer bookmarks, and Todd had his in the Tom Clancy book he had been reading in Rome the week before. Part of the prayer that intrigued Todd was the line in which Jesus taught us to ask God to forgive our trespasses, or sins, as we forgive those who trespass against us. When Lisa told me Todd had prayed that particular prayer, I felt certain that, in some way, Todd was forgiving the terrorists for what they were doing.

Following the prayer, Todd recited the 23rd Psalm. *Yea, though I walk through the valley of the shadow of death, I will fear no evil. . . .* Other men apparently joined in with him or

[6]See Matthew 6:9-13.

recited the psalm themselves. Interestingly, Psalm 23 wasn't a mantra Todd recited often, but it was resident in his spirit because he had learned it as a child. When the crisis came, Todd was able to tap into a deep reservoir of faith that he'd been storing up for years.

Lisa Jefferson recalls, "After that, he had a sigh in his voice, and he took a deep breath. He was still holding the phone, but I could tell he had turned away from the phone and was talking to someone else. He said, 'Are you ready? Okay. Let's roll!' "

It was nearly 10:00 A.M. EDT. The plane was 15 to 20 minutes away from Washington, D.C.

Jeremy said to Lyz, "Hang on the line. I'll be back." Lyz couldn't bear to listen, so she handed the phone to her dad.

"They're doing it!" he said.

When I allow myself, I can picture it. . . .

From the rear galley of a 757 to the front cockpit area is a distance of more than 100 feet. . . . Big men move quickly up a narrow aisle, accompanied perhaps by a flight attendant or two carrying coffeepots, spilling boiling water on themselves as they run. Some jump over seats to get as much manpower to the front of the plane as possible. A food cart is used to ram the enemy.

All around the airplane is filled with screams and commotion.

Flight attendant Sandy Bradshaw is on the phone with her husband, Phil. "I have to go," she tells him. "We're running to first class now."

Elizabeth Wainio, who has just borrowed a cell phone from another passenger, is talking with her stepmother. "I have to go," she explains, cutting her call short. "They're breaking into the cockpit. I love you. Good-bye."

CeeCee Ross-Lyles is on the phone with her husband, Lorne, when the screaming starts. "They're doing it!" she yells. "They're doing it!"

Just what they were doing or how they were doing it may never be completely known. The cockpit voice recorder contains sounds of dishes shattering and other objects being hurled. The hijackers are heard screaming at each other to hold the cockpit door.

Someone cries out in English, "Let's get them!"

One of the hijackers frantically attempts to cut off the oxygen in order to quell the passengers' fight. Another of the terrorists tells his cohorts, "Take it easy."

Pounding sounds on the cockpit door . . . a male passenger shouts. . . .

More screaming!

The plane begins to dive.

The hijackers shout, "Allahu akbar!" God is great!

Papers rustle within the cockpit as the hijackers begin fighting among themselves for the plane's controls. "Give it to me!" one of them commands. Too late.

The plane rocks from side to side and then flips over before streaking straight down, blasting a hole in the earth 50 feet deep. Thousands of gallons of burning jet fuel spray the trees, instantly scorching the tree line as though a raging forest fire has recently been put out.

The airplane is obliterated. . . .

Yet United Flight 93 had not crashed into the Capitol; nor had it smashed into the White House, Camp David, or any other national landmark. Instead, it crashed at 10:03 A.M. on September 11 in an open field with only a stone cabin nearby and the closest home more than a quarter of a mile away.

■ ■ ■ ■

Meanwhile Lisa Jefferson remained on the line, waiting for Todd to come back. Hearing all the commotion on board the plane, she recalls, "Then it went silent. I didn't hear anything else from him. I kept the phone line open for about 15 minutes, hoping he would come back to the phone. I called his name, but he never came back to the phone. About 10 minutes later we heard that a plane had crashed near Pittsburgh, and I knew that was his plane. It was United Flight 93.

"When I took off the headset that morning, I felt that in the 15 minutes we had together, Todd and I had bonded as good friends. . . . I felt like I had made a friend for life, and I felt that I had just lost a friend."

I told Lisa that no doubt Todd had felt the same way. Then I thanked her for being such a rock for Todd, a comfort for him and for me. And I thanked her for the wonderful gift she had given my family and me with the news of her conversation with Todd. When Lisa told me about Todd saying, "Let's roll!" I had to smile. That was "so Todd."

"He said that?" I asked her to be certain.

"Yes, he did. He said, 'Are you ready? Okay. Let's roll!' " Lisa repeated.

They were Todd's last words.

"That's his phrase," I said. "We use that phrase all the time with our boys. When they hear, 'Let's roll!' they head for the door. They know what it means, sort of 'Let's get ready for the next thing we're going to do.' And Todd said, 'Let's roll!' "

Interestingly, Lisa told me it was a miracle that Todd's call hadn't been disconnected. Because of the enormous number of calls that day, the GTE systems overloaded and lines were being disconnected all around her as she sat at the operator's station outside of Chicago, talking to Todd. She kept thinking, *This call is going to get dropped!* Yet Todd stayed connected . . . all the way to the end.

The calls describing what happened aboard Flight 93 meant so much to me and to millions of Americans. The courageous actions of the passengers and crew reminded me that on a day when people around the world felt violated, helpless, alone, and afraid, there were still people of character, people who in the midst of crisis dared to live to the last second with hope. Truly the valiant heroes aboard Flight 93 fought the first battle in what President Bush declared as a war against terrorism . . . and won.

21

SAYING GOOD-BYE TO TODD . . . FOR NOW

RECEIVING THE INFORMATION from Airfone operator Lisa Jefferson regarding Todd's call from Flight 93 brought relief in many ways. For the first few days following September 11, anyone who talked with me for any length of time usually stepped gingerly around the awkward questions: "Well, what do you think Todd did? What do you think his role was?"

Most of our family members and friends who knew Todd well had already assumed that if anyone had mounted a counterattack in the air, Todd would have been involved. We knew that in our hearts. But nobody wanted to say such a thing for fear of sounding boastful, naive, or both.

When Lisa Jefferson provided factual information that Todd had indeed been involved, it was a wonderful blessing. But it was also the beginning of an entirely new saga in our lives.

Obviously we were not the only people to learn of Todd's heroic and inspiring words and acts. Other people now knew of his last words, "Let's roll!" Many people were calling Todd a hero.

A hero? He was always a hero to us; certainly David and Drew had always thought of their dad as a hero. Todd's sisters and family members always regarded him as a hero. So did my brothers, especially Jonathan, who looked to Todd as a mentor and someone he strove to emulate. And Todd was the love of my life. But a hero? Like Abraham Lincoln, Jesse Owens, or Michael Jordan? Like John Wayne, Tom Landry, or Billy Graham? Was Todd a hero like them? Most of our American "heroes" in recent years have been film stars, athletes, or musicians. The term *celebrity* seemed to apply more appropriately to them than *hero.*

In my lifetime, only since September 11 has our country once again taken to regarding firefighters and police officers as heroes—men and women who willingly place themselves in danger to help save others. The Bible verse, *Greater love has no one than this, that he lay down his life for his friends* (John 15:13) began showing up in public places. Interestingly, the statement was originally made by Jesus the night before he gave up his life willingly, not only for his friends but also for his enemies.

Now the whole world was referring to the passengers and crew of Flight 93 as heroes. And news-media representatives from every place imaginable were calling *me* for comments and interviews about my husband, the hero! It was both humbling and overwhelming.

The first interview I accepted was in our home on the Saturday night following the September 11 events. The *Pittsburgh Post-Gazette* had been one of the main sources of information on Flight 93, since the crash had occurred about 80 miles southeast of Pittsburgh. While other national media attention focused on New York and Washington, the *PPG* had done herculean work at covering the crash in Shanksville. So when their representatives called and asked if I would speak with them, I gratefully consented.

A Philadelphia television news team came to our home to interview me that same night. As I went upstairs to change my clothes for the interview, I thought, *What am I doing?* I didn't know anything about dealing with the media. I'd never done major press interviews in my life! I didn't have anyone coaching me as to what I should say or not say.

So I had no choice but to be myself. I didn't try to present myself in any particular manner. I simply answered the reporters' questions as best I could, as honestly and straightforwardly as I knew how. When I didn't know the answer to a question, I simply said so.

In those mind-numbing days after the crash I had (and still have) no desire for publicity. I did, however, hope that by doing the interviews I'd have some small public record of who Todd was and some documentation of what he had done aboard Flight 93 . . . for the sake of our children. Little did I know that I'd eventually have miles of videotape and stacks of printed materials for our kids to examine someday.

I also realized early on that one of the best ways for me to get information about Todd and Flight 93 was through the media. As helpful as United Airlines was, no doubt they also had a plethora of legal advisors instructing them to be careful about giving victims' families too much information. And the government agencies were still investigating, so trying to get information from them was equally difficult. But the media somehow was able to penetrate both bastions and pull out valuable information. It wasn't always accurate, but it was usually intriguing. So as the reporters interviewed me, I interviewed *them* for every tidbit of information I could learn about Flight 93.

I quickly discovered that there were extremely professional, sincere, accurate reporters in the business, and there were those who were less so. Some media with whom I did interviews had most of their story written before they ever talked with me. Others took a grain of truth and twisted, planted, or spun it any way they chose. For instance, one paper said that my learning about Todd's call "made my life worth living again."

While I appreciated the sentiment, anyone who knew me immediately recognized that I had not made that statement. My life, like Todd's, is worth living because of my relationship with God. I had plenty of reasons to live, long before learning about Todd's call—including two young boys and a baby on the way. So while learning about the call was a tremendous blessing, it was not my reason for living!

Knowing about the call did, however, create a slightly different emphasis during our memorial service for Todd, lightening our spirits. We had planned to celebrate his life and influence anyhow. The fact that he was now known to have played a role in preventing Flight 93 from killing any more people on the ground simply was another example of the Todd we had always known.

Nick Leonard, our United Airlines representative, helped immensely in arranging flights for relatives trying to get to New Jersey in time for the memorial service planned for Sunday. Two relatives flew in from Jamaica. Others drove hundreds of miles to be with us. Todd's dad arrived on Saturday evening after driving more than 3,000 miles to be with us and attend the service. In all, more than a thousand people showed up at Princeton Alliance Church on Sunday afternoon to honor and remember Todd—and the news of his involvement with Flight 93 had not yet been splashed all over the national media.

During the memorial service I was still rather shell-shocked. Throughout most of the service I sat in the front of the sanctuary, staring and smiling at a picture of Todd we had placed in front of the pulpit. Everyone involved with the memorial concurred that we wanted it to be a respectful remembrance of Todd. Beyond that, we wanted to celebrate both his life on earth and the fact that we knew he was enjoying the presence of God in heaven, even as we wept for him here. It was also an expression of our family's and friends' faith that we would one day join him. I wanted the memorial to be an accurate portrayal of who Todd was—a balanced presentation that said, "Yes, there's a lot of sadness and sorrow here, but there's also a lot of joy here." As Christians, we mourn, but we do not mourn as those who have no hope.[7] Consequently, not only did we want to say *who* Todd was but also *where* he is, and the joy that he knows today.

From the start, when people recognized Michele Beamer

[7] See 1 Thessalonians 4:13.

playing the prelude at her own brother's memorial service, it was obvious that this wasn't going to be a "normal" wake. The opening Scripture reading was the one Todd had last quoted, Psalm 23, followed by the Lord's Prayer. My brother Paul read a paraphrased version of Todd's conversation with Lisa Jefferson, information that many in the room were hearing for the first time.

Paul shared some personal thoughts about Todd, and then my 18-year-old brother, Jonathan, spoke of Todd's influence in his life. Pastor Cushman presented a nutshell version of the gospel Todd believed and the faith by which he lived . . . and died.

A video collage comprised of photographs of Todd throughout his lifetime was shown, accompanied by the recorded music of Keith Green, who died in a plane crash in the prime of his life and ministry.

Then friends and family members offered special thoughts about Todd. The guys from the Care Circle and the Friday-morning breakfast group stood on the platform together, each one sharing memories of Todd. Every person who spoke added some meaningful insight into the person Todd was. Their words were both marvelous to listen to and excruciatingly painful at the same time.

In perhaps the most poignant statements of the day, David Beamer, Todd's father, voiced what many people in the room were thinking. "We serve the one and true God. Todd and his newfound friends on that Tuesday morning— new freedom fighters is what they really were—did the right thing. . . . Certain faces of evil were on that particular plane. Of course I have said to myself many times, 'Why was our beautiful son on that plane?' But we know why he was on it. The faces of evil, those particular hijackers, they picked the wrong plane. . . . Actions of Todd, and the other young men and women . . . thwarted that part of the mission. . . .

"While we are grieving . . . and also celebrating Todd's life . . . I must confess that as Todd's father, I take a certain comfort in knowing that in some other parts of the world . . . the forces behind this evil, the planners who plotted it and were ready to celebrate complete victory, are having their own remembrances today. They are not celebrating in the street about either the Capitol or the White House being taken out. I also know with certainty that the hijackers did not have the name of Jesus on their lips in their final moments. And it is now a fact of the matter that they know they didn't only pick the wrong plane. They picked the wrong side."

Todd's dad concluded, "I am not saying that Todd was perfect. But I can say for Todd's family, there could be none finer, none more ideal. So Todd, thanks for all you were while you were here. You certainly represented your family, your Christian brothers, your God, and our country very well."

David then prayed a prayer that touched our hearts. "Almighty God, thank you for Todd Beamer. . . . Thank you again for your precious gift, your Son, Jesus Christ, who died for us. Heavenly Father, I have known what that meant, but it is only in these recent days that I have a little more understanding of how it felt.

"I thank you so much that our son, Todd, has the prom-

ise of eternity because of the gift of your Son. . . . Also . . .
we pray, heavenly Father, that Todd's witness and his
actions can be used to your glory in the things that matter
most."

Following the "amen," David paused and offered one
last expression of faith. "I have one more thing," he said.
"God, please bless America . . . and Todd, we will see you
later."

22

THE SHANKSVILLE CRASH SITE

OVER THAT FIRST WEEKEND we talked frequently with our United Airlines family liaison, Nick Leonard. At one point, Nick mentioned the possibility of visiting the location where Flight 93 had crashed in Shanksville, Pennsylvania, a small town in Somerset County southeast of Pittsburgh. My first response was "Nope, no way! I'm not going. I don't need to see that." Originally we had received word that we might be able to visit the site on Friday, but then the FBI refused to grant permission. I didn't mind. I wasn't even sure I wanted to visit the site, but a number of victims' families were asking United to arrange such a visit. As I thought about it, I concluded, *If I don't go now, I probably never will, and I may regret it someday. If I go, it can't be much worse than what I've already experienced, so if the opportunity arises, I'll go.*

United was able to arrange a trip to the site on Monday, September 17. The airline provided vans and drivers to take us from Cranbury, since Todd's family was still in town for the memorial. Joe Urbanowicz, our longtime family friend, and George Pittas, one of Todd's Friday-morning buddies, accompanied us as well. In all, about 35 people from our family made the trip. We loaded up before dawn, around 5:00 A.M., and headed across the Pennsylvania Turnpike. I slumped into the seat behind the driver and tried to sleep along the way.

Why am I doing this? I thought. *What do I hope to see? Am I going to be able to handle it? Or is it going to be the final straw that sends me over the edge?*

Prior to the trip, I had received instructions from the coroner's office in Pennsylvania that I was to bring along DNA samples if possible, to be used in trying to match any remains found at the site. Mom and I went around my home looking for anything of Todd's that might provide DNA samples—hair in a hairbrush, a fingernail clipping, any fibers that might reveal DNA. We tried to maintain a sense of dignity as we carried out this surreal chore, looking at each other from time to time as if to say, *How weird is this?*

It was around ten o'clock by the time we arrived at Seven Springs Ski Resort, a large hotel in the area that had become the command center for the federal and local investigators as well as for the hundreds of members of the national and international media. National Guardsmen were visible throughout the hotel. As we walked by, the various military, Pennsylvania state police, and other law-enforcement personnel saluted us. It was an odd feeling—after all, who were we to be saluted? But I appreciated the gesture, as did other family members. All day long, wherever we went, officers saluted.

At the hotel we were directed to a security checkpoint, then ushered to some tables where the coroners were collecting our DNA samples. Todd's parents gave blood samples and filled out a pack of forms for identification purposes. It was a bizarre scene. But when I stepped up to the table with Todd's samples, my eyes connected with the woman who was filing everything. She expressed such concern and compassion that I knew instantly she shared our hope and our faith. She didn't have to say a word; her very countenance radiated the love of God. She took us to another building and worked with us in a private room as she gathered the information she needed. She told us that she was part of an on-call coroner team brought in from Texas to help at the crash site. She told us she was praying for all the Flight 93 families and would do everything possible to return our loved ones' remains to us. The coroner's team, led by Wally Miller, the local Somerset County coroner, kept their promise and cared for us and our lost loved ones with compassion and dignity over the months ahead. Amazingly, every family from Flight 93 eventually received remains and the knowledge that in some small way their loved one had come home.

From Seven Springs we boarded a motor coach, along with other victims' family members, for the 35- or 40-minute trip to the crash site. I had seen the site on television shortly after Flight 93 had crashed, and it had left an indelible impression on my heart and mind. Now, as the bus drew closer to the location, I could feel my stomach starting to churn.

Along the way we passed through several little towns,

and the people of Shanksville and the surrounding area stood alongside the road in a silent salute. A few waved as we passed by, but most of them simply stood there reverently. Many of them held homemade signs offering condolences and promising to keep us in their prayers. It was an incredibly moving sight, and many of us in the bus were fighting back the tears. Others didn't even try. In the center of Shanksville, a few minutes from the site, someone had erected a large placard with the names of the passengers and crew aboard Flight 93 who had perished as a result of the terrorists' hijacking. The kind expressions of condolences and grief from this tiny, obscure community, which had suddenly become a focus of national attention, were humbling and moving tributes.

It was small-town America at its best. By now, news of what had happened aboard Flight 93 was spreading rapidly. Although the people were sad that this tragedy had happened in their backyard, they were also proud to be associated with the flight of heroes who had prevented further destruction and chaos in our country.

When we arrived at the site, I was surprised at how ordinary it appeared. It looked more like a construction area than the site of a plane crash. Large machinery sat alongside the actual crash site, and men in white hazardous-materials suits still scoured the grounds.

The plane had come down in an open field, an area that had once been a coal strip mine and since had been reclaimed, graded, and replanted. Off in the distance I could see a farmhouse, but there were no buildings anywhere else for miles. Silently I thanked God for that.

Compared to the horrific scenes of devastation at Ground Zero and the Pentagon, this place seemed almost serene.

The federal authorities wouldn't allow us to get too close to the actual spot where the plane had struck the ground, but they took great care to describe it for us and to answer any questions about how they believed the plane had come down. The spot where the plane had hit was ashen in color and looked like a large, bloated cross in the ground.

I didn't see a single piece of airplane anywhere. The authorities said that they had found a few engine parts, one large piece in a pond about half a mile away, and some small fragments about the size of a notebook. Other than that, the plane had totally disintegrated. Tiny pieces of plane debris were embedded in the trees surrounding the site. More than 400 rescue workers had combed the area searching for fragments or anything that could identify victims. Little could be found. Because of the reclaimed strip mine, the ground was softer than other surrounding areas. The plane had pierced the earth like a spoon in a cup of coffee: the spoon forced the coffee back, and then the coffee immediately closed around the spoon as though nothing had troubled the surface. Anything that remained of Flight 93 was buried deep in the ground.

At the top of a bluff overlooking the site, a makeshift altar area had been constructed from several bales of hay. Two small flags and one large flag were stuck in it. A cross with white bunting was on the side of the hay-bale memorial.

We had been told in advance that we would be able to place wreaths, flowers, notes, pictures, or other personal items at the crash site memorial area, so following the brief ceremony, as tears streamed down our faces, family and friends placed their offerings on the hay-bale altar.

As my special mementos of Todd, I left an Oracle pen, a Chicago Bulls cap, some pictures of Todd and the boys, a container of M&M's (one of Todd's favorite candies), notes from family members expressing our love and how proud we were of Todd and how we hoped we would make him proud of us, too, and a book, *A Life of Integrity* by Howard Hendricks, that Todd and the guys had been using in their Friday-morning breakfast group. I had thought of leaving a Bible, but I didn't feel comfortable leaving a Bible out in the elements.

It was a sunny September day, close to 70 degrees. As I gazed out over the site one last time, I saw a hawk soaring high in the sky above the field where the plane had crashed. Suddenly a sense of peace flowed over me. I couldn't explain it, but I was reminded of Isaiah 40:30-31:

> *Even youths grow tired and weary,*
> *and young men stumble and fall;*
> *but those who hope in the Lord*
> *will renew their strength.*
> *They will soar on wings like eagles;*
> *they will run and not grow weary,*
> *they will walk and not be faint.*

Never before in my life had the difference between those who put their hope in God and those who put their hope in this world been so obvious to me. Following

September 11, I saw firsthand many dear people who were trying their best to cope with loss, hurt, anger, fear, and a host of other feelings. Some had lost a husband, father, daughter, mother, or friend. They wanted to soar like eagles; they deeply desired to get on with life. They wanted to look on the bright side and do the things the clichés recommend, but they didn't have the strength. Worse yet, they had no *hope*. My family and I mourned the loss of Todd deeply that day . . . and we still do. But because we hope in the Lord, we know beyond a doubt that one day we will see Todd again. I hurt for the people who don't have that same hope, and I pray that somehow the events of September 11 will encourage them to investigate the possibility that faith in Jesus really is the answer to all of their life questions.

We remained at the crash site for about an hour. I hardly spoke to anyone at the site. Most of the victims' families kept to themselves in their mourning and didn't interact. Afterward we went to a memorial service at another location a few miles away. There we were greeted by various members of Congress and other dignitaries from Pennsylvania, including Governor Tom Ridge. The first lady, Laura Bush, was the special speaker for the ceremony. She offered sincere words of condolences and encouragement to each family member, then spoke to us briefly. "I want each of you to know today that you are not alone. We cannot ease the pain, but this country stands by you. We'll always remember what happened that day, and to whom it happened."

Several others expressed noble sentiments. "From this

moment forward, just let there be peace with all of us, and love," one woman said.

I couldn't help but compare this service to the one in Plainsboro the day before. Todd's memorial service had been so uplifting, so inspiring, because the emphasis had been on the hope that God provides, especially in the midst of crisis. On Monday, as I listened to the well-intentioned speakers, who were doing their best to comfort but with little if any direct reference to the power of God to sustain us, I felt I was sliding helplessly down a high mountain into a deep crevasse. As much as I appreciated the kindness of the wonderful people who tried to encourage us, that afternoon was actually one of the lowest points in my grieving.

It wasn't the people, or even the place. Instead, it struck me how hopeless the world is when God is factored out of the equation. My brother Paul noticed it, too. A deeply compassionate man, he later said, "It was heart-wrenching for me to see people grieving without hope. I've never seen a more vivid illustration of the truth: We mourn but not as those who have no hope."

When we got back to the hotel, where we were to meet our airline driver, a television producer asked if I would answer some questions on camera. I was tired, weary, and ready to collapse, but I did the interview anyhow. I later learned it was for *Inside Edition*, a nationally syndicated show.

We traveled all the way back to New Jersey that same night, getting in about 2:30 A.M. I was glad I had gone, but it's a day I'd never want to repeat.

When I got home, I found two delightful surprises. First,

our Care Circle had cleaned the house from top to bottom while we had been away. That may seem insignificant, but the house had been overrun with people visiting till late Sunday night after the memorial service; then we had left early Monday morning. For a neat-nik such as me, to walk back into the house after such a difficult day and find it all cleaned and put back together was a tremendous gift.

Second, I found several new outfits in my clothes closet. Since I was pregnant, I had a limited wardrobe of maternity clothes, most of which were jeans and T-shirts or informal summer clothes. But I had consented to do several interviews in New York the following morning, so my friends had gone out and purchased some new maternity clothes for me to wear. They even ironed them and left them hanging neatly in my closet.

I quickly packed a few things for the New York trip, and David Beamer, my friends Doug and Chivon MacMillan, and I tumbled into the car. We arrived in the city around 4:00 A.M. and slept for about an hour before the 5:00 A.M. wake-up call to get ready. It was going to be another long day.

23

IT'S JUST ME!

WHEN I TOLD TODD'S STORY on national network television news shows on September 18, I hoped many people not only would realize what had happened aboard Flight 93 but also would understand the person Todd was. But I never could have guessed the impact of the story on all of America—or the world.

I was so tired and overwhelmed by the events swirling around me that there was no way to prepare in advance, even if I had wanted to. I could only say, "God, help me. I don't know what I'm doing here. It's just me. I have nothing to say to the world. But for some reason, here I am. I am totally dependent on you." Chivon's constant prayer for me during my interviews was that God would fill my mind with his Word and the things that he wanted said in each situation. Indeed, at several points during the many interviews I did, I felt as though I were watching and listening to someone else. I'd hear my voice speaking and then stop and think, *Who said that?* Clearly God was guiding my thoughts and words in ways I could hardly imagine.

One of the first interviews I did was on ABC's *Good Morning America*, with Diane Sawyer. Also on the show that morning was Lyz Glick, Jeremy's wife. We met for the first time before the program, and the moment we saw each other, we forged an instant bond. We had a lot in common. Not only are we about the same age and live in the same area of the country, we were both married to sports nuts who were doting fathers and were now being hailed as heroes. Indeed, as the reports confirmed what had happened aboard the flight, it became more clear that Jeremy and Todd were instrumental in formulating and carrying out the counterattack. Other men and women were involved as well, but because of Jeremy's and Todd's prolonged phone calls, more information is available about their thoughts, words, and actions. Lisa Jefferson summed it up well: "They were all heroes. They all pitched in and did what needed to be done."

I wore a new blue blouse and a dark skirt, thanks to my friends in the Care Circle. Neither Lyz nor I had ever anticipated being in this position. We reached across the chairs on the television set and held hands as Diane Sawyer introduced the segment by telling the audience of Todd's and Jeremy's actions aboard the flight. She mentioned that they and others on Flight 93 had been recommended for Medals of Freedom, the nation's highest civilian honor.

We reviewed the details of Jeremy's and Todd's calls, their last words, and their involvement during the final moments of Flight 93. Diane picked up on Todd's phrase, "Let's roll!"

I explained to her, as I would to so many others in the

weeks and months ahead, "As soon as I heard those words, I knew that it was Todd." That phrase was something Todd said all the time around our house. We often used it with our little boys. "It's hard to corral them sometimes, so we say, 'Come on, guys. Let's roll!' That means, let's head to the door, let's get our shoes on, let's go out and do what we need to do. So when I heard that phrase, I knew that it was Todd's cue, saying, 'We're going to do what we need to do here; let's put our best foot forward.'"

Diane told the audience that I would be having a baby in January, then asked what it meant to me that I could tell our children what their dad did.

"For the first three days after the crash, I didn't know what Todd's role was," I answered. "Everyone asked me, 'What do you think he did?' I said, 'I know Todd; he wouldn't sit back and allow something like this to happen to other people and to himself. He was a competitor, and he would have fought it.' And now we have the concrete evidence of his character that I can pass on to all three of my children. People can tell them how great their daddy was, and now we can show them how great he was. That's a great legacy for them to have . . . and for me to hold on to . . . and I have held on to it these past seven days."

At the close of the interview, as the cameras pulled out of the shot, Diane, the consummate professional, expressed gracious thanks. Throughout the morning she was extremely kind to Lyz and me, helping us through the nerve-wracking and emotionally charged interviews.

Following the "live" interview, Diane taped extended segments with Lyz, David Beamer, and me for *Primetime.* At breakfast, in between *Good Morning America* and *Primetime,* I met Emmy Glick, Lyz and Jeremy's 12-week-old baby. Seeing Emmy reminded me how our baby would look in just a few months, how vulnerable these little human beings are, and how much responsibility I now had. As we parted, Lyz and I vowed to keep in touch, which we have done.

Later that day, David and I taped a long segment with Stone Phillips of NBC's *Dateline.* Stone, like Diane, was obviously personally touched by the story of Flight 93. I felt confident he would use our words to paint a picture of how much influence even "little people" can have when they act with character, faith, and courage.

At dinner with Doug, Chivon, and David, we were talking about mundane, normal things . . . when it suddenly hit me: nothing in my life would ever be normal again. How vastly different life was from just a week ago! I felt as though I might burst out bawling at any second, so I hastily excused myself and retreated to my hotel room. Chivon followed closely behind me, and once inside the room, the two of us broke down and wept. We prayed for peace in our hearts, and for strength and wisdom.

That night I was scheduled to be interviewed on CNN's *Larry King Live,* which airs on the East Coast at 9:00 P.M. Although Larry King was broadcasting from Los Angeles, I was taken to the CNN studio in New York. My already low energy level was dwindling even further, and Larry's hour-long program that evening was packed full. I was scheduled to be the last guest on the roster, following King Abdullah and Queen Rania of Jordan; New York City's esteemed mayor, Rudy Giuliani; former New York governor Mario Cuomo; former Maine senator George Mitchell, who was in Washington; and from Florida, Lorne Lyles, husband of CeeCee Ross-Lyles, one of the flight attendants aboard Flight 93.

Mayor Giuliani was rushed in right before airtime. He had been at Ground Zero and was going right back after the show. Only the mayor, Governor Cuomo, and I were in the studio in New York; the other guests were located elsewhere. As we waited in the "greenroom," I was privileged to meet and talk with Mayor Giuliani after he went on the air. He made a point to hug me and to express how proud he was of the heroes aboard Flight 93, and how determined he was to help everyone get through the nightmare. Like most Americans in the midst of the crisis, I was deeply impressed by the mayor's indefatigable courage and resiliency. He exuded a sleeves-rolled-up, let's-get-it-done spirit. His we'll-get-through-this attitude was contagious.

Unfortunately, I didn't get to hear much of Mayor Giuliani's interview with Larry King. While waiting to go on, I sat down in the greenroom next to former governor Mario Cuomo and . . . fell asleep! My snooze wasn't a political statement; I was tired, pregnant, and plain wiped out!

I was still rubbing the sleep out of my eyes when the producer asked me to take my position for the interview. A gifted interviewer, Larry King treated me as though I were every bit as important as the king and queen of Jordan or the vaunted mayor of New York. Besides asking me questions about the details of the crash and my conversation with Lisa Jefferson, Larry threw the door wide open for me to discuss Todd's and my faith. "You're not surprised, then, at the prayer?" Larry asked.

"Not at all," I responded. "Todd was a man of faith. He knew that this life is not all there is, that this life is just to prepare him for eternity in heaven with God and with Jesus. Todd did his best every day. He wasn't perfect and neither am I. But he did his best to ensure that he was living a life that was pleasing to God and would help him know God better, and he acted on that all the way to the end."

Larry mentioned David and Drew, and the fact that I was expecting our third child. The implicit question was, "How are you handling it? What are you going to do?"

I told Larry, "Sometimes people look at me and wonder, 'Is she in shock? Or is she unrealistic about what the situation is?' They don't see me all the other times when I'm breaking down and losing my composure. Certainly, the faith that I have, like Todd's, helps me to understand the bigger picture here. And that God's justice will ultimately prevail. We have more to look forward to than just what we see here on earth."

"I admire your faith and your courage," Larry said. "You've given a lot of people a lot of hope here tonight." The program closed with the national anthem sung beautifully by Larry King's wife, Shawn, while the screen flashed images of the valiant efforts of firemen, police officers, and volunteer rescue workers amidst the rubble of what had formerly been the World Trade Center and the Pentagon.

The studio was almost empty by the time David, Doug, Chivon, and I left the building and stepped out into the warm September evening. A full week had passed since the attacks on our nation, and smoke was still drifting skyward from Ground Zero.

■ ■ ■ ■

Back home on Wednesday, we had long since passed the point where somebody wanted to pick up the telephone when it rang. Doug MacMillan became the official phone screener, almost by default. The phone rang constantly, even more so after I had done the television interviews. Well-wishers and more interview requests kept the lines hopping. But then came a most surprising call.

John Vandenheuval, a Wheaton College graduate and now the chief of staff in the office of Representative J. C. Watts from Oklahoma, called and invited me to attend the president's address to the nation in Washington, D.C., the evening of Thursday, September 20. In addition to offering his personal condolences, John indicated that he was also calling at the behest of Dennis Hastert, the Speaker of the House of Representatives.

"Sure," I said, rather naively. Who would turn down such an invitation? I was still running on sheer adrenaline, not having had a good night's sleep in more than a week, so I felt as though I was in a fog. "Go hear the president? Sure, why not?"

Once again, I was faced with a decision about what to wear. I didn't have time or the desire to go shopping, and the new outfits my friends had purchased for my New York trip were more casual clothing. I realized that I didn't even *own* a formal maternity dress, or anything that might be appropriate to wear to a speech by the president of the United States to a joint session of Congress!

Elaine Mumau had come to the rescue when I had faced a similar situation on the previous Sunday for Todd's memorial service. "I have a friend who had a baby in August, and I think she's about your size," she suggested. "I'm pretty sure I saw her wearing a simple but sophisticated-looking black dress. I know she'd let you borrow it."

"Do you really think so?" I asked.

"Of course!"

So I borrowed the dress for the memorial service and again for the presidential speech.

I was officially invited to the presidential speech by the Speaker of the House of Representatives, Dennis Hastert, whose office made all the arrangements for me to attend. Doug and Chivon, my traveling partners, agreed to go along again on yet another trip. We made the three-hour drive from our home in New Jersey to the hotel in Washington where we planned to stay overnight. All the way there we kept looking at each other in disbelief, as if to say, *Is this really happening? We're actually going to the Capitol as guests of a congressman.* It would have been a wonderful experience had it not been for the circumstances that brought us there.

Doug and Chivon weren't planning to attend the president's speech. But when we arrived, we discovered that Dennis Hastert had included them in our invitation, and they would be sitting right behind me!

We also found another surprise invitation waiting for us. Congressman Watts had invited us to dinner. Doug,

Chivon, and I looked at each other in amazement. This was too unreal!

We went out to dinner at Union Station with Congressman J. C. Watts, John Vandenheuval, and some friends. Had I not known that J. C. Watts was a congressman, I never would have guessed he was a politician. A former pastor, he was a kind, unassuming, soft-spoken, humble man who truly had an interest in serving rather than being served. Not once all evening did the representative proclaim his achievements in Congress or toot his own horn in any way.

Congressman Watts, John Vandenheuval, Doug, Chivon, and I went from dinner to the Capitol. As we approached the building that night, with its magnificent rotunda all lit up, it was an awe-inspiring sight. I couldn't help wondering what would have happened if Todd and the other "freedom fighters" aboard Flight 93 had not taken the actions they had. Would this historic building even be here? Moreover, would many of the people who worked at the Capitol still be here? Seeing the Capitol still standing brought home the true value of the sacrifice Todd and the others had made.

Not surprisingly, security was extremely tight even though we were entering with a congressman. Congressman Watts took us to Dennis Hastert's office and introduced us to the Speaker of the House. A photographer snapped some shots as the Speaker and I shook hands. I assumed that I was just there for a quick "photo op" and would be shooed into another area to await the president's speech. After all, as the Speaker of the House, Dennis

Hastert was in a position to know much more about the gravity of the president's speech than most people. No doubt he could have easily spent the minutes leading up to the speech besieged by any number of important political figures or the media.

Instead, the Speaker spent more than 20 minutes talking with me about Todd's life, our faith, and the events that brought us to this evening. We stepped out on the veranda overlooking the Washington Mall as we spoke, and I was reminded afresh of what the heroes of Flight 93 had saved.

Before we knew it, one of Speaker Hastert's aides indicated that it was time to head for the House Chamber to hear President Bush's speech. The aide led Chivon, Doug, and me through the hallways of the Capitol and up to the door. Just before we entered the Chamber, the aide said to me, "When the president addresses you, you can stand up and acknowledge him; you can wave, curtsy, bow, or whatever feels comfortable to you."

I was completely unprepared for the fact that the president even knew who I was, let alone that he would include me in his speech. *You've gotten me this far, God,* I thought. *I'll trust you for this, too.* That stopped the butterflies in my stomach as I entered the Chamber.

I was seated in the lower balcony next to Joyce Rumsfeld, wife of Donald Rumsfeld, the Secretary of Defense. Mrs. Rumsfeld was kind and almost motherly toward me, offering her condolences and asking about my children and how they were doing. She told me how she and her husband had been enjoying retirement after serving on President Bush's father's staff, but when George W. Bush had called, they had felt they needed to respond for the good of the country. She was so friendly and warm, it didn't occur to me until later that Mrs. Rumsfeld's husband was the very man who now needed to track down and bring to justice the terrorists who had perpetrated the heinous crimes about which the president was prepared to speak.

Although I was still very much mired in my own sense of devastation, it was nonetheless awe-inspiring when the room was called to order and the sergeant at arms called out, "Ladies and gentlemen, the president of the United States."

President Bush entered quickly and in a very business-like manner. The crowd of U.S. senators and congress-people and their guests rose instinctively in a standing ovation. It was obvious that an unusual unity pervaded the room; our nation had been attacked, and partisan politics had been replaced with a spirit of cooperation unlike anything our nation had seen in the past 60 years.

President Bush made his introductions and launched into his speech. I settled back as best I could and focused on listening to what the president had to say. This was an important speech for our nation; it would set the tone for our response to the terrorist attacks that had taken more than 3,000 lives, including the man I loved, the father of my children. I wanted to hear what the president planned for us to do.

"In the normal course of events, presidents come to this chamber to report on the state of the union," President Bush began. "Tonight, no such report is needed. It has already been delivered by the American people. We have seen it in the courage of passengers who rushed terrorists to save others on the ground. Passengers like an exceptional man named Todd Beamer. And would you please help me to welcome his wife, Lisa Beamer, here tonight?"

The room erupted in applause.

I was shocked! When the aide had mentioned that the president might acknowledge my presence, I thought he might make some passing references to Todd and Flight 93. I was amazed that he would do so in such an overt manner at the beginning of this most significant speech.

The entire Congress of the United States of America rose to its feet in one motion, so almost instinctively, I rose as well. The Congress applauded and applauded, and it was the most humbling experience of my life to know that they were applauding me, in an indirect effort to express their appreciation to Todd and the other heroes aboard Flight 93. I was overwhelmed.

Standing there in my borrowed dress, with the eyes of the whole world on me, I somehow managed to remain standing. I even offered a discreet nod to the president of the United States and the Congress. Mrs. Rumsfeld and Connie Clark, wife of Chief of Naval Operations Admiral Vern Clark, who had been sitting on my opposite side, both stepped back and were smiling and applauding. I could hear Doug and Chivon applauding behind me. I glanced down at the floor of the Chamber and saw the faces of our national leaders looking back up at me, applauding. It was an extremely strange feeling.

No doubt if Todd were alive, he'd be laughing and saying, "Can you *believe* this?"

I sat down as though in a dream, and the president continued, "We have seen the state of our union in the endurance of rescuers working past exhaustion. We've seen the unfurling of flags, the lighting of candles, the giving of blood, the saying of prayers in English, Hebrew, and Arabic. We have seen the decency of a loving and giving people who have made the grief of strangers their own. My fellow citizens, for the past nine days the entire world has seen the state of the union, and it is strong!"

The Congress rose to its feet again in applause, as it did many times that night. Each time I pulled my pregnant body up out of the seat and applauded as well. President Bush's speech was masterful—firm yet filled with hope—and the response of Congress was not the polite applause sometimes deemed appropriate at bipartisan functions. Quite the contrary: this was America's statement to the world that we were indeed the *United* States. It was an incredible, historic experience, and I felt so honored to be there on behalf of Todd and all the other passengers, crew, and families of Flight 93.

When the president's speech concluded, the room emptied rather quickly, as many senators and congressmen had statements of their own to make in response. I stood up carefully and spoke briefly with Mrs. Rumsfeld, thanking her for making me feel so welcome. Other people came over to say hello and shake hands, and I greeted them.

Suddenly we heard applause rising again from the lower floor of the congressional chamber. Mrs. Rumsfeld took my hand and gestured for me to look down. I peered over the balcony railing and there, down on the floor of the congressional hall, were dozens of congressmen and congress-women, clapping their hands and looking up . . . at me! I realized it was their way of expressing their heartfelt gratitude for what Todd and the others had done . . . that, in a real way, the passengers and flight attendants on Flight 93 might have saved not only a national landmark but also the lives of our national leaders. Once again I was overwhelmed and humbled by the most gracious actions of the congress-people.

It was a bittersweet sensation to be introduced by the president of the United States and given a standing ovation by the U.S. Congress. Even more so when the president referred to Todd as "an exceptional man." I was still trying to make sense of it all as we walked outside and started down the Capitol steps.

I had agreed earlier in the day to be a guest on CNN's *Larry King Live* following the speech, so a producer whisked us down a few subterranean halls. Soon I was waiting in line behind Senator John Warner and Senator Kay Bailey Hutchison to share my thoughts on the speech with Larry. We did a live interview right from Capitol Hill.

Once again Larry King seemed awed by the story of Flight 93 and was extremely complimentary and kind in his comments to me.

"What did it feel like?" Larry asked, after showing a clip of my being applauded by the Congress.

I answered off the top of my head. "It felt amazing. I had already known that what Todd did and the other guys did . . . their ultimate sacrifice . . . was not in vain. But to see the Capitol Building standing here tonight and to have so many people look up and say, 'Thank you, because I was in the Capitol that day' was such an encouragement to me."

Larry King asked me to review the call from Lisa Jefferson again. Then he led into several spiritually oriented questions. "How are you holding up?" Larry asked. "I know there's a part of this with all the attention and the heroics involved, but you said that it was your faith that [gets] you through, right?"

Chivon must have been praying, because I just opened my mouth and said, "That's right. I know that Todd's death was not in vain. I see evidence of it all over as people have come up to me saying what an inspiration his faith and my faith have been to them. I just hope that it leads to a revival of faith in this country and the world. It's clear that that's what we need right now. It is time for that in our country."

Larry asked, "You seem to be dealing remarkably with your grief. How do you explain that?"

"I know that Todd is in heaven right now, and I know that I'm going to see him again, and that his efforts were not in vain. It was part of God's plan. Evil in this world will ultimately be conquered by God. . . . That's something I can hang on to during those moments when I'm not cool, calm, and collected, of which there are many, I can assure you."

I did several other interviews following the president's address, with almost all the interviewers asking me what I thought of his speech. The next morning I was a guest on *Good Morning America* again. It was crazy! *And you want my opinion?* I thought. *It's just me! I'm a mom and a housewife from a small town in New Jersey.* Certainly at times I felt awed that these highly intelligent, politically astute people were asking *my* opinion about what the leader of our country had said! But mostly, I just answered the questions as best I could.

I knew Todd was laughing in heaven!

■   ■   ■   ■

Back home, I attempted to reestablish some sense of routine and normalcy in life for David, Drew, and me—as much as that was possible.

We had missed David's first day of school on September 10, and life was a blur following September 11, so when I finally took David to preschool, I tried my best to make it seem normal for him. "Mommy is dropping you off, and I will be picking you up after school," I told him. David had been looking forward to this day, and I wanted him to enjoy all the usual excitement associated with starting school.

The first day of school can be an emotionally charged, traumatic time for a child—not to mention a parent—so I walked in with David to help get him situated in his classroom. I didn't really know anyone there, but as we walked up the stairs, I noticed people looking at me. I thought, *All I want to do is drop my child off at school on his first day, smile at him, and kiss him good-bye. I want to get through this without breaking down and bawling. I just want to be a normal mom.*

David's teachers, Mrs. Edwards and Mrs. Iorio, met him at the door and made him feel welcome. We looked at each other knowingly, but nobody referred to anything that our family had experienced. They treated David just like all the other kids, which was exactly what I had hoped. Before long, he joined right in with the other children.

A few months later, at David's first parent-teacher conference, one of his teachers told me, "If I didn't know what had happened in your family's life, I would never know by how we see David act every day."

That was one of the most wonderful things she could have said to me. I had done everything I could to ensure the boys felt as much love and security as possible since September 11, and it was paying off. I know there will be pain for them to deal with in the future, during many stages of their lives, but I'm trusting God to help us deal with that when it comes. For now, seeing them laugh and play like all is right in the world is the best thing I can imagine.

24

POIGNANT
MOMENTS . . . AND
KEY DECISIONS

GETTING LIFE BACK to "normal" was much easier said than done. A few days after the president's speech, I received another call from Washington. The president had invited all of the surviving family members of Flight 93 to come to the White House for a private, unpublicized meeting on Monday, September 24.

My mom, Paul, Jet, and I made the trip, as did Peggy, Michele, and David Beamer. Nearly 400 people gathered at the White House, all of whom had lost someone close to them in the crash. Conspicuously absent were members of the media. President and Mrs. Bush wanted to meet with the family members outside the glare of the television lights and the telephoto lenses.

First, President Bush spoke kindly and compassionately to the entire group in the East Room of the White House. He used no notes and spoke from his heart, almost conversationally. Then he and his wife, Laura, moved to an adjacent room, where they took time to meet with each family individually.

The president and first lady met with our family for about eight to ten minutes, greeting each one of us and offering words of encouragement. In a rather refreshing twist, President Bush didn't offer the usual condolences, such as "I'm sorry for your loss," or something similar. Instead he offered words of praise and appreciation, thanking us for the way we were handling the situation dropped in our laps as a result of September 11. As he spoke, however, his eyes were moist with tears.

My brother Paul spoke briefly with the president. "I just want you to know," he said, "that our family is praying for you."

"Thank you," President Bush said. "I know that you are, and I really appreciate that."

When the president greeted my mom, he nodded toward me. "You brought up a good one." My mom is usually very unassuming, but I could tell she was proud of that compliment. In my family's opinion, Mom deserves lots of awards for her parenting.

Before leaving the White House, the president's staff photographer took a picture of our family with President Bush. Nothing like having the president of the United States in your family photo album! Yet the president and first lady made us feel so comfortable, we felt like neighbors. They seemed in no rush, taking time with each person.

At the conclusion of our visit, the families all walked out through a long White House hallway. In preparation for us, the White House staff had lined both sides of the hall in a sort of makeshift honor guard, clapping their hands for us as we walked by. Many of the staff members had tears in their eyes. It was a heartfelt gesture, and we were deeply moved as we passed by.

Beyond the president's kind and inspiring words, the fact that he would take the time to meet with us in the midst of such a serious crisis spoke volumes to our family. The president had met with Tony Blair, prime minister of Great Britain, earlier that morning before coming in to greet the family members, and he had a full schedule of high-level meetings following the sessions. Yet in the midst of a national crisis, the president took nearly three hours to meet with the family members of Flight 93. And to do so with no media attention was an extremely meaningful and uplifting statement to our family.

■ ■ ■ ■

We've always had lots of family pictures around our house, so in an effort to keep Todd's memory fresh in the minds of our children, and to let them know that it was okay to talk about their dad, I had several of our favorite family photos enlarged and framed. I placed them in locations at the boys' eye level. For instance, I put several pictures at the base of our fireplace, just to the side of the hearth. I put more pictures on low nightstands and other places where the boys could see them easily.

I wanted the boys to feel free to talk about Todd, so I brought him up in conversation whenever I could. "Remember when you and Daddy fixed that lamp together?" "What do you think Daddy would say about your gymnastics show?" "Here's the basketball Daddy bought for you." Sometimes it felt forced, but mostly it was just natural—Todd *is* still part of our family and always will be. His influence will live on for decades in me and in our children.

A reporter also passed me an unbound book that allows a child to fill in descriptions of his favorite things as well as some of Daddy's favorite things. David and I filled in his book together, talking about Todd as we completed each page. Then I filled in Drew's copy, so he can compare his likes and dislikes with those of his daddy someday. I even made one up for the baby.

My brother Paul made a promise to me following Todd's death. Similar to Joe Urbanowicz's commitment to our family after our dad died, Paul promised, "Lisa, I'm going to be an important person in your children's lives. I'm going to be there for you and the boys." And he and his wife, Jet, have done that, although it has been emotionally wrenching at times.

One weekend in early October, Paul, Jet, and my mom visited the boys and me in New Jersey. Paul played with David and Drew all weekend, and the boys had a ball with their uncle. On Saturday we went to a pumpkin farm where each person picked out his or her own pumpkin.

At the close of the day, coming back home, I drove and Paul sat in the front passenger seat; Mom and Jet were in the middle seat, and the boys were in the backseat of the van.

David suddenly called up to Paul. "Uncle Paul, you could be my daddy, right?"

The silence in the vehicle was almost palpable. I stared

straight ahead, afraid to turn my head toward David for fear I might burst out in tears. Paul, too, kept his eyes glued to the road in an attempt to hide the tears streaming down his face.

Finally Mom came to the rescue. "Well, Uncle Paul can't be your daddy, but he can do a lot of things with you that your daddy used to do."

"Okay," David piped up from the back of the van. That was all he needed to hear.

■ ■ ■ ■

In mid-October I received a phone call from Kathy Tedeschi, one of the women who had lost her husband in the terrorist attack that brought down Pan Am Flight 103 in Lockerbie, Scotland, 13 years earlier. We talked briefly, and I could tell that she understood some of the hurt, frustration, and questions I lived with on a daily basis. Kathy described her desire to form a support group for people in the Princeton area who had lost loved ones in the September 11 attacks. She invited me to the group's first meeting the following week.

Many of the towns in our area had lost someone on September 11. Lorraine Bay, one of the flight attendants aboard Flight 93, was from Hightstown, where Todd and I had lived in our first house. LeRoy Homer, one of the pilots, also lived nearby. Most of the victims, however, were commuters who went to work at the World Trade Center on September 11 and never returned home.

I had never been part of a support group before, and I

didn't know what to expect. I soon discovered, though, that people who were once complete strangers can become the most trusted of confidantes. We share a unique and painful experience that even our closest friends and family can't thoroughly understand or help us through sometimes. Before long this group became an important part of my healing; our meeting was something I looked forward to as an oasis in my week. A friend from the group and I share the same birthday, so we decided to have dinner together that night. We both noted that one of the unexpected blessings of this tragedy was the opportunity to meet people whose paths we never would have crossed otherwise, and count them as friends. It's another thing to be thankful for.

In meeting with other victims' families through the support group and other contacts, I was struck again and again by how many young children, and even yet-to-be-born children, had been left without one parent or another on September 11. In that respect, this tragedy was unprecedented in our nation. At the same time, since the nation had heard Todd's name, I began receiving mounds of cards, letters, and checks from well-wishers from coast to coast and from many nations.

We were inundated with songs, poems, and essays that people had written especially for David, Drew, the baby, and me. We received toys for the boys and all sorts of gifts for the baby—stuffed animals, blankets, and clothing. I received enough inspirational books and CDs to start a small library! There were pins, hats, and shirts piled high on my dining-room table for months. By such gestures I've become convinced that the American spirit of compassion and generosity is alive and well. A few families even named their new puppies "Beamer" and sent us pictures of the dogs.

Two servicemen—one a Vietnam veteran and one a veteran of World War II—sent Purple Hearts that they had earned in battle.

I was awed at the generosity of people who didn't know me, had never met me, and had no contact with me apart from seeing me on television or reading an article. While grateful for their sentiments and gifts, I was uncomfortable accepting contributions for my family alone when there were so many other families who were hurting, too.

From the beginning I was extremely cognizant of the fact that there were many unnamed heroes on September 11. Each child who lost a parent lost his or her personal hero. Yet of all the people who died that day, most of us can only name a handful. After talking with some friends in our Care Circle, I decided it was wisest to set up a nonprofit foundation through which donations could be funneled to many of the families. I was especially concerned about meeting the needs of the very young children—needs that may not appear for years, after the spotlight on September 11 is dim and the support services are gone.

The Todd M. Beamer Foundation was established in October 2001 to address these concerns. Doug MacMillan put his career in medical sales on hold to come on board as the director of the Foundation. Another good friend who attends our church, Bill Beatty, is an accountant and vice president at Goldman Sachs. Bill took a leave of absence from his job to help set up the accounting and financial structure of the organization. That in itself was a tremendous step of faith for both Doug and Bill, as none of us had any idea just how much money would come in to the Foundation, for how long, or how quickly it would be dispersed. Doug had talked with Todd frequently about possibly making a career change, so when the need collided with the opportunity, Doug answered the call.

We spent the next several months doing the legwork to properly set up the Foundation, including filing with the IRS for 501(c)(3) status, which establishes the Foundation as a nonprofit corporation. This holds us to a high standard of accountability for fund management, including exempting my family from benefiting, thereby removing any potential for conflict of interest. Todd always did business with the utmost integrity, and I wanted to be sure that the Foundation bearing his name would do the same.

Many people have contacted the Foundation saying, "We want to do something to help the victims and promote the sort of values that Todd represented, but we don't know what to do or how to do it." Doug has helped guide their fund-raising efforts, making sure that the methods used to raise the money are appropriate and respectful to the victims of September 11, and that the money raised goes to the right places and is used properly.

In addition to setting up operations, Doug and Bill have also coordinated numerous meetings with churches, civic groups, and businesses that want to contribute. A meeting with one such potential donor set up one of the most bizarre events in my life since September 11.

25

THE "COMPLETED" FLIGHT TO SAN FRANCISCO

BILL BEATTY and Doug MacMillan had been in contact with Oracle, keeping them posted on what we were doing with the Todd M. Beamer Foundation. They arranged a meeting with some Oracle executives at the end of October to present the mission and plan for the Foundation. When they told me they had scheduled a meeting, I said, "Maybe I should go along. After all, I know a lot of people at Oracle, and Todd and I both worked for the company. The presentation might be better received from me than from someone else." Doug and Bill were delighted that I was willing to go with them, so they set about making the arrangements.

Our meeting was scheduled at 1:00 P.M. the next day, at Oracle's corporate headquarters in Redwood Shores, near San Francisco. United Airlines offered us free travel, so we scheduled the first flight out of Newark, United Airlines Flight 84, leaving at 8:15 A.M. It never crossed my mind, at first, that the flight we had scheduled was the replacement flight for Flight 93, whose flight number was, of course, discontinued following the crash.

Booking that particular flight was not done as a gimmick by me, by the Foundation, or by United Airlines. Nor did I look at flying to San Francisco as a particularly courageous act. I had no fear of flying, and with the increased security in place, I felt it was probably safer to fly now than ever. The fact that the flight was so similar in routing to the one Todd had died on was coincidental. It was the one flight that would accommodate my schedule.

But then the media got word of my travel plans, and before we even realized the significance of our trip, newscasts heralded the story that "the widow of Todd Beamer, one of the heroes of Flight 93, was completing his flight." Almost immediately more media requests came pouring in.

I briefly considered canceling my plans or changing the flight to avoid all the melodrama. Then I recalled President Bush's encouragement in one of his speeches: that it was time for the country to get on with our lives, to get back to normal as much as possible, and to do those things we ordinarily would do. To cancel the trip would be handing a victory to the terrorists who had attacked our country. It would send a wrong message to the American public: that I was reticent about air travel—which I was not. The only reason I wouldn't have gone would have been an irrational fear of flying, or, more specifically, fear that the terrorists were going to strike again. And I was not about to allow myself to be held captive by fear of any kind.

Early on Friday, October 19, Doug, Bill, and I headed for

the airport. As we drove up the New Jersey Turnpike to Newark International that morning, I couldn't help wondering what Todd had been thinking and seeing as he drove the same route on September 11. I could imagine him driving in the dark with the radio on in the background as he talked on his cell phone or picked up voice-mail messages, with no clue as to what was about to happen. With a little smile I wondered if he had heard the announcement on that day's sports report that Michael Jordan intended to come out of retirement. I'd relived that morning so many times in my mind that I thought I'd become almost numb to it. But as we approached the airport, we swept past the long-term parking lot, and an emotionally charged memory caught me by surprise.

The last time I had been to the Newark airport had been September 10, when Todd and I had returned from Rome. The day we departed I had dropped off Todd and our bags at the terminal and then parked our car in the long-term lot. So when we arrived back in Newark, I had said, "Why don't you stay here with the bags, and I'll go get the car and come back to pick you up?"

Now, as we passed by, I saw the exact spot where Todd had waited for me. That was hard enough, but it evoked a multitude of other images. I could almost see Todd and me pulling into the curbside check-in areas, and it suddenly hit me how many times Todd and I had flown out of this airport. I thought of all those things we did as a team. I could almost hear him saying, "Okay, I'll drop you off with our bags, and I'll go park the car." Now Todd was no longer there to do those things he'd always done so willingly. And then the truth smacked me in the face: despite the help of wonderful people around me, I was basically on my own.

Doug and Bill and I disembarked at the entrance to the United check-in counter. It was still dark outside when we checked in, but members of the media had gathered already. As we did an impromptu press conference right at the check-in area, I asked myself, *What am I doing!?* It was another surreal moment to add to the long list since September.

"Okay, we have to go now," Doug said, leading me by the arm away from the reporters and back outside to the parking lot. Various network television feeds had been arranged so the networks could all interview me from the same location. The television camera crew gave me an earpiece through which I could hear the interviewer speaking to me. I stayed in the same spot and worked with the same cameraman and crew. The only thing that changed was the person to whom I was speaking.

"Okay, you'll now be talking with Matt Lauer of NBC-TV," I heard in the earpiece. I did the interview with Matt, and then a minute later, I heard, "Okay, we now have Jane Clayson from CBS," and suddenly I was talking with Jane. "We're ready for Diane Sawyer of ABC."

"Okay," I said, and went on to talk with Diane. Next was Paula Zahn from CNN. Most of the interviewers asked similar questions: "Why this flight?" "Why now?" "Are you afraid to fly?" "Will you be reliving memories of Todd?"

The massive media coverage was actually a twofold blessing. It provided information about the Foundation to many people who might not otherwise have heard about it. And it certainly distracted me from sitting and pondering the last moments Todd might have experienced at the Newark airport.

When I was done with the interviews, a United Airlines supervisor took us around the ticket lines and hustled us right to the front of the security-check line. The security officer scanned and checked my carry-on bag; I wasn't carrying much since we were only staying overnight. Once through security, I stepped to the side to wait for Doug and Bill behind me. As I glanced at the long line, I thought it must have been quite similar about this time the morning of September 11, as Todd opened his computer for the security check and placed his phone in one of the plastic containers to go through the scan. Little did he know that also going through these lines were four men who had devised a method of beating the scanning machines, whose carry-on luggage contained box cutters or knives. Looking around at the other passengers, there was no way I could tell—anyone in the line could have been a terrorist.

Doug had a small fingernail file on his nail clippers that caused the alarms to go off. The security guard made Doug break the blade off his nail clippers before clearing him.

We walked down the long corridor leading to the gates; it was lined with glass on both sides. Glancing outside, I saw the United Airlines Boeing 757 jet that would whisk us to California. I could imagine Todd passing by the T.G.I. Friday's restaurant at Terminal A, Gate 17, on the morning of September 11, and I wondered, *What were those four other men doing? The men who had no intention of going to California?*

United Airlines had closed Gate 17 for a month following the crash, and employees had placed a lone U.S. flag at the end of the jetway in silent honor of the men and women on board Flight 93.

We boarded Flight 84 from a different gate. I walked directly to my seat on the plane and tried to be inconspicuous as I buckled my seat belt. It didn't bother me as the plane's engines revved to a roar and we raced down the runway. Perhaps if Todd's death had been due to a mechanical failure or pilot error, I might have gripped the armrest a bit more tightly. But as we swept into the sky, I had no fear. When I looked out the window, however, I couldn't tear my eyes away from the fabulous Manhattan skyline . . . missing the World Trade Center towers. A deep sadness momentarily overwhelmed me for the thousands of families who were starting out their activities this day, missing a loved one.

During breakfast, I noticed that the airlines had replaced all the metal knives with plasticware. It occurred to me that if someone really wanted to harm another person, a fork could do damage as well. I recalled Jeremy Glick's remarking to Lyz that he still had his butter knife and joking that he might be able to use it as a weapon against the terrorists aboard Flight 93.

As we were commenting on the plastic knives, I quietly quipped to Doug and Bill, "I guess it's good that they took away the knives and your fingernail file. But you could really hurt someone with a fork or a glass, if it was broken and you used the shards!"

Ironically, five minutes later, one of the flight attendants in first class dropped a glass, leaving large, pointed shards on the floor.

"Look at that!" I whispered in mock terror to Doug.

Truth is, as much as the airlines and the government do to improve security on board airliners, subway systems, cruise ships, or other public transportation, our best efforts are not fail-safe. In some ways, there is no true security anywhere in our world. Tall buildings are vulnerable, and tunnels, nuclear plants, public stadiums, and other large public places will always have a level of danger. The only true security in this life comes from placing our trust in the God who loves us and is in complete control of the events of our lives and our world. At a memorial service for Todd conducted at Wheaton College, President Duane Litfin summed it up when he said Todd had learned the lesson of martyred missionary Jim Elliot, who lived by the adage, "When it comes time to die, be very sure that all you have to do is die."

The actual flight to San Francisco was relatively uneventful except for the short period of time when we passed over Cleveland. Flying at about 35,000 feet, I had a sickening feeling in my stomach as I thought, *It was right about here that the terrorists took over the flight and turned it back toward Washington.* I blinked hard, took a deep breath, and settled back in my seat for the remainder of the flight.

When we got off the plane, we were met by another bevy of reporters. More significantly, we were met by a large contingency of United Airlines employees standing in the gate area, applauding. At first I thought they were simply acknowledging Todd's part in preventing Flight 93 from hitting Washington, but then I realized the wider picture. I had never considered the ramifications of my travel on the employees, but apparently they saw my trip as a welcome endorsement in a time when many people were reluctant to fly. The idea was, "If Lisa Beamer isn't afraid to fly on our airline, you can trust us, too."

Beyond that, the country's response was overwhelmingly positive. Although I hadn't considered my actions as brave, others did. I guess it encouraged people to be reminded, once again, that even though the terrorists had taken much from us, we still had strength and resolve to conquer our fears and reestablish our lives. That much of the melodrama was definitely true: I had indeed decided that with faith in God, my children and I could face whatever life brought to us, and we'd do so as a testimony of Todd's faith and our own.

■   ■   ■

I had flown once before this since 9-11, although not commercially. Oprah Winfrey had invited me to appear on a show featuring some of the miracle stories of September 11. I didn't think I was ready to travel commercially yet, so at first I declined. Then Oprah's show offered to send her private jet to New Jersey to pick me up and bring me home. Doug and Chivon accompanied me, and I made the trip.

Approaching Chicago from the east evoked deep emotion. Coming up on the city, I looked out the jet's window and saw the Sears Tower. I recalled going up the tower with Todd while dating and then later celebrating our five-year wedding anniversary in downtown Chicago.

Another emotional moment came when I met Lisa Jefferson backstage at Oprah's show. Although we had talked on the phone, this was our first meeting face-to-face. We had seen each other's pictures on television, so we each knew what the other looked like. No one needed to introduce us; we recognized each other immediately. We smiled, hugged, and shed a few tears as we greeted one another warmly and Lisa introduced me to her husband, Warren.

On the show, Lisa and I reviewed the details of her 15-minute conversation with Todd. It seemed as though it was the 10,000th time we'd told the story in the past few weeks. We kept thinking that maybe next time the story would have a happier ending. But it never did. If there's a happy ending, it will be that people will be inspired to their own small acts of faith and courage every day as a result of hearing what Todd and Lisa Jefferson said and did that day. She will always be a hero to me.

Two young men were on Oprah's show because of what they had done at the World Trade Center on September 11. As they were hurrying down the stairwell after the first plane had hit the building, they met up with a woman in a wheelchair. Rather than leave her to die, they picked her up *in her wheelchair* and carried her sixty-some stories down to the ground. They got separated in the confusion, and after the collapse of the towers, they were uncertain what had happened to the woman. Later they discovered that they had indeed saved her life, and she was able to express her thanks. They were strong young men who could have gotten out much more quickly by themselves, but at great risk to their own lives, they carried the woman in the wheelchair to safety and to another chance at life.

In a way, that's what Todd and the other heroes aboard Flight 93 did for some people in Washington. And in a way, that's what Lisa Jefferson did for me, as well. I couldn't possibly thank her enough. In a gesture I wholeheartedly supported, Chicagoans voted her "2001 Chicagoan of the Year."

26

THE REASON
FOR MY HOPE

THROUGHOUT THE FALL OF 2001, there were many difficult logistics to deal with, as there are with all loved ones' deaths—filing forms, finding documents, canceling credit cards, and sorting through personal items. One of the most painful for me was dealing with Todd's car. It had been parked at the airport on September 11 and was impounded, along with the cars of all the other passengers and crew of Flight 93. The authorities were searching for information or *anything* that might lead to the identification of the terrorists, whose cars had also been parked at the airport.

When the car was available for release, I didn't want it brought back to our house right away. I was concerned that the boys would see the familiar white sedan coming down the road and think Daddy was home. Brian and Elaine Mumau volunteered to have the police deliver it to their house temporarily. When the car arrived, I asked if they would go through it and put Todd's personal belongings in a box that I could sort later.

They agreed and tackled the sad job. I'm sure they threw away gum wrappers, coffee cups, and gas receipts as they packed up his sunglasses, CDs, suit coat, notebook, and Bible. One item they found, however, was intriguing. In the armrest tray between the front bucket seats, Todd had some Scripture memorization cards that he used while driving. The top card on the stack, the one that he might have read on September 11, was Romans 11:33-36:

> *Oh, the depth of the riches of the wisdom and knowledge*
>   *of God!*
> *How unsearchable his judgments,*
> *and his paths beyond tracing out!*
> *"Who has known the mind of the Lord?*
> *Or who has been his counselor?"*
> *"Who has ever given to God,*
> *that God should repay him?"*
> *For from him and through him and to him are all things.*
> *To him be the glory forever! Amen.*

It was the exact passage of Scripture that had helped me through my questions following my dad's death; the same passage I'd been reminded of at Wheaton College; and the very passage that had been my memory verses for the Bible study I was preparing in Rome, the week before Todd died. Seeing that card reminded me that God is always speaking to us and giving us just the words we need for the events he knows lie ahead.

■ ■ ■ ■

Even in the midst of heart-wrenching responsibilities, I
tried to do many of the things I would have been doing if
September 11 had never occurred. One of these was attending a conference, scheduled for early November, with
women from our church. I had registered to attend Women
of Faith back in May, thinking it would be fun to get away
with my friends for a weekend and leave Todd and the
boys at home to fend for themselves.

It was a short drive to the Core States Arena in Philadelphia, and nearly 130 women from our church planned to
join about 25,000 other women for two days of speakers and
music meant to encourage us in our faith. None of us ever
imagined when we made our plans in May that *I* would be
on the platform.

When the sponsors of the event discovered that I was
attending, they asked if I would share a few words with the
audience. I had wanted to remain as inconspicuous as
possible, but Mordecai's rejoinder to Esther—"Who knows?
Maybe God has you here for such a time as this"—echoed
through my mind. I agreed to say a few words.

The emcee introduced me, saying, "Since the events of
September 11, many have questioned the love of God. But
many who know him well have not. One person in particular
has not questioned his love. Her name is Lisa Beamer. . . ."

The crowd of women burst into applause as I walked
onto the platform. They kept clapping and clapping, to the
point that it was embarrassing. Just by scanning the faces in
the crowd, I knew some of these women had faced far

worse circumstances than I had. . . . Who was I to talk to them?

I confessed to them that I had originally signed up to get away from my husband and kids for the weekend.

"At that time in May," I said, "September 11 was just another date on the calendar for all of us. Now, when we hear that date, it brings to mind all sorts of things, from fear to anger to sadness to—for the thousands of people in my shoes—thoughts of all the loss that we have experienced personally. We're left with choices about what we will do with those feelings. The choices for people like me—and for many of us in this room—are to look at all the things we've lost or to look at all the things we have; to become bitter or to become better; to live in fear or to live in hope.

"I've chosen to live in hope. . . ."

The crowd interrupted me with a burst of applause, which I appreciated, but I didn't want anyone to misunderstand the source of my strength. "The reason I've been able to do that is not because I'm a strong person. I don't want anyone to go out of here thinking, *Wow, she's so strong; look at her!* The reason I've chosen to live in hope is because of the heavenly, eternal perspective God has given me. That tells me that fear comes from feeling out of control, and if September 11 has taught us anything, it is that we are never really in control. Todd and I were two people who planned for the future; type A's who had all our ducks in a row. And yet we were not in control on September 11.

"But hope comes from knowing who *is* in control. Hope comes from knowing that we have a sovereign, loving God who is in control of every event of our lives. . . . In the book of Jeremiah (29:11) it says that God has a plan for me, a plan to prosper me and not to harm me; a plan to give me a hope and a future. And that is what holds me together every day when I get out of bed in the morning: to know that is true, and it has been proven true in my life to date. It was true on September 11, and it will be true for as many years as God has left for me, and for whatever he has in store for me . . . and for my children.

"It's a time of uncertainty, and many people are looking for something to cling to. I hope for you that you can cling to the one who has all the power, and all the love, and all the care, because he's the one who's really in charge."

The "Women of Faith" gave me another rousing standing ovation and sent me soaring home on a cloud, with my faith built up. Good thing, too, since over the next few months my faith was going to be sorely tried in the nitty-gritty of daily living. We were about to enter the "mean" season, the season of birthdays and holidays . . . the first without Todd.

27

LIFE GOES ON . . .
OR DOES IT?

THEY SAY THAT life must go on . . . and I suppose it does whether we want it to or not. But when you've lost someone you dearly love, you know that life will never really be the same.

The boys and I went to Mom's for Thanksgiving. I was reminded of wonderful family times together, as well as my husband's birthday and our engagement day—the day he asked me to marry him, high atop Turkey Mountain—all in the same weekend! Now the view from Turkey Mountain had been transformed; the World Trade Center towers formerly seen in the distance were gone . . . and so was Todd.

Similarly, we had difficulty maintaining some of our family traditions. For instance, Mom didn't put the corn kernels out on the Thanksgiving dinner plates this year. We did express our thanks to God, but she just couldn't bring herself to put out the kernels. Maybe next year . . .

I didn't want to be the focus of everyone's attention or

have our whole day filled with sadness. But as we got closer to dinnertime, I knew I wasn't going to be able to hold my emotions in check. So I went to my room by myself to cry for a while. I knew my feelings of grief and loss had to come out, and after they did, I felt a little better. Even so, dinner was difficult, and I spent more time gulping back tears than enjoying the turkey and trimmings that Mom had made. Although Thanksgiving was a special day on the calendar, this year it was like most of the others lately—filled with the horrendous sadness of missing Todd but also with the recognition that there is still much to be thankful for. The image of the sun shining behind a black rain cloud seemed the best illustration for my feelings. That night I was happy to crawl into bed, knowing that the first of many holidays without Todd was behind me.

I knew I couldn't handle another of our favorite Thanksgiving traditions—going out together as a family to cut down the Christmas tree. Each year it had always been an all-day affair, with Paul and Jet, Holly, Jonathan, Mom, Todd, the boys, and me selecting and cutting down our trees and taking them home atop our cars. This year Mom and the family waited till the boys and I left and then went out to the tree farm.

The emotional pain of going through Todd's birthday on November 24 and the reminder of our engagement was almost more difficult to deal with than Thanksgiving.

I wasn't sure how to handle it. *What should we do?* I wondered. I wanted to honor Todd's birthday for the boys' sake as well as Todd's, but I had no clue how to make it special without making it morbid.

Then it came to me. For my birthday that year, one of the presents Todd had given me was a Ticketmaster gift certificate. Our summer had become so hectic that we'd never used it for a Broadway show, as Todd had intended. *Toy Story on Ice* was playing at the Meadowlands Arena on Todd's birthday, so I thought, *Why not? That's a good way to use that certificate. Todd would have liked it.* The boys and I went to the show, and it was wonderful. I actually enjoyed it.

But in the car on the way home, the reality of what this day could have been hit me again. Tears streamed down my face. David noticed and asked, "Why are you so sad, Mommy?" I attempted to explain. "Mommy is sad because Daddy isn't with us on his birthday," I said, wiping the tears from my eyes.

In his inimitable innocence, David looked up at me and asked, "But, Mom, we can still have cake, can't we?"

For a moment I wasn't sure whether I was going to burst out laughing . . . or bawling. Finally I gulped hard and choked back the tears. Then I said with a smile, "Yes, David. I guess we can." How grateful I was, again, for a little child's perspective!

I told the boys, "I think Daddy would be happy that we spent his birthday with Buzz Lightyear." We all agreed.

■ ■ ■ ■

I knew that getting through the Christmas season was going to be difficult. The first challenge was getting the Christmas tree with the boys. The first Saturday in December, I went to a lunch with my friend Sharon Vogel while her husband, Brian, took the boys out to the golf course. Afterwards Brian said, "Hey, we're going to go get our Christmas tree today. Would you and the boys like to come along?"

I had been planning to pick out a tree that day anyhow, but I wasn't certain how I was going to accomplish the task on my own. Brian's invitation solved that problem.

I said, "Sure!" It was an unseasonably warm December day, with the temperature over 70 degrees as we went to a Christmas-tree farm down the road from our house. We picked out our trees, and Brian cut them down and threw them in the back of his pickup truck. The tree farm had a "sleigh ride" with a Santa Claus on a hay wagon. "Come on, guys, we're taking a hay ride with Santa Claus!" Sharon called out. We all piled in the hay wagon and had a great ride through the fields, singing "Jingle Bells" in our Bermuda shorts in the bright, warm sunshine. The whole experience was so different from anything we'd ever done before, it was impossible to compare it to past Christmas trees we had gotten with Todd. That made it easier.

Brian hauled the tree in and put it in a stand for us. The following morning, David and Drew and I got out the Christmas ornaments and started putting them on the tree. When David asked me why I was crying, I showed him all of Daddy's ornaments—many of which I had given to him, or he to me, on special occasions such as our trip to Disney World or some special sports event. We had a habit of buying an ornament from every place where we

traveled together. Each ornament held immense significance to me and represented a piece of our life together.
Each brought to mind special memories, which I related to
the boys—for as long as they would listen! I look forward
to telling them those stories every year so they can pass
them on to their own children someday. David made sure
that the ornaments would see another Christmas by
reminding me to place them strategically on the tree.
When it was time to hang Todd's glass Chicago Bulls
ornament, David told me, "Mom, you need to put that one
up high, so Drew doesn't break it."

In the busy weeks of December, I did another interview
with Larry King, and it aired on Christmas Eve. I told
Larry, who by now seemed very familiar, "It's definitely
hard when you get out the Christmas tree and the decorations, and you find ornaments that were Todd's. And you
look at pictures from last year and think how it should be,
or how it could be."

Nevertheless, I was committed to making Christmas as
special and normal as possible for the boys. A few days
before Christmas, we loaded up the minivan and drove to
my mom's in Shrub Oak, New York, for Christmas. Then
we went back home to New Jersey, reloaded the car, and
went to visit Peggy and David Beamer in Washington, D.C.,
the day after Christmas. Whew! I was worn out!

Walking into the house where Todd and I and the boys
had shared so many wonderful moments with Todd's
family was another heart-wrenching experience. I hadn't
been back to the Beamers' home since the White House visit
following the events of September 11. That day, when we'd

stopped at their house to pick them up on the way, I'd burst out in tears.

Now it was Christmas, and I knew it was bound to be a strange experience for all of us. Even just having me show up at the Beamers' door with their grandsons, and being pregnant with Todd's and my third baby, would be a bitter-sweet reminder for them as well as for me. Nevertheless, I knew David and Peggy loved me as their own daughter, and we were all committed to maintaining the same relationship we'd always had.

The boys and I arrived the evening after Christmas and knocked on the front door. I thought, *Okay, I can do this. I don't need to break down crying.* Melissa's husband, Greg, met me at the door. I walked into the kitchen and saw Todd's parents while the boys darted downstairs to play with their cousins. As much as I tried to hold back my tears, I couldn't. I just started bawling all over again.

We had a great visit together, opening gifts, eating, hiking in the woods with the kids, and all the usual Christmas celebrations. The family stoically attempted to hold in our tears. For the most part we succeeded. Then, as we were leaving, Peggy and Greg helped me get the children safely buckled in the car. I started pulling the minivan out when David suddenly said, "Mom, stop. I forgot to tell Uncle Greg something."

"Okay, David, but hurry up, please." We pulled back into the driveway and there were Peggy and Greg, crying quietly together. David happily finished his conversation with Uncle Greg, but we were reminded again of the immense sadness we all felt.

■ ■ ■ ■

We celebrated David's fourth birthday at The Little Gym, a gymnastics center, on January 5, just four days before the baby was to be born. We had 20 guests, pizza, and a Buzz Lightyear cake (of course!). Celebrating David's birthday without Todd wasn't as hard as I thought it might be. I just got caught up in the kids' joy. Certainly I missed Todd, and yes, if I allowed myself, I could easily dwell on the past or mourn the present. But David and Drew were having a wonderful time; why should I dampen their spirits?

I had reason to feel good. I had made it through the holidays, Todd's birthday, and David's birthday. Besides, I had another "birth day" coming up in just a few days. It loomed larger in my mind than the holidays, birthdays, or any other stressful time we had encountered since September 11. For me, this would be the ultimate challenge.

28

WELCOMING
MORGAN

AS METICULOUS PLANNERS, Todd and I had anticipated
our first two children; the third pregnancy took us by surprise. Nevertheless, we were thrilled when we found out I
was pregnant with our third child. Then, following the
upheaval in our lives after September 11, being pregnant
became one of the most nagging conundrums. It was one
of the most difficult aspects of "life after 9-11" for me to
understand. Todd and I both believed that children are a
blessing from God. Yet profound questions rankled my
mind . . .

*God, since you know the end from the beginning of the story,
why this baby? Why did you allow us to become pregnant when
you knew Todd wasn't going to be here to see this baby grow up?
Why is this baby coming into a world where he or she will never
truly know his or her father, will never see Daddy's smile, hear
his voice, or be lifted high in the air and hear Daddy say,
"Wheeee!" Why a baby with a missing parent?*

Even from a logistical standpoint, I wondered how I

was going to make it. I could handle two children by myself. I'd often done so when Todd was away. Two children was doable; I have two arms and two hands, so everything matched. But three children can be a challenge even with two parents. I couldn't think about how it was going to work with just me.

I knew the only answer was to trust God to provide everything I needed. I'd had a recent example of his faithfulness even in the little details of life. Because of our unusually warm December, I had an unexpected opportunity to get some yard work done before the chill of winter set in. Even though I was eight months pregnant, I decided I had no choice but to tackle the weeding and trimming. So one Saturday I took the boys out and let them play while I put on my gardening gloves and attempted to reach around my big belly to pull the weeds. About an hour later, I compared how much I had accomplished with how much remained to be done, and I realized that I'd hardly made a dent. The simple chore of pulling weeds overwhelmed me. I fretted over my inability to get the job done now . . . or ever!

I looked over at the boys, and the nagging worries caught me again. *How am I going to raise them—and one more—by myself?* I began crying quietly as I continued to slowly tug at the weeds and had almost stopped work altogether when I heard a vehicle approaching. I looked up to see a Jeep pulling into our driveway. My friend Jan Pittas got out and called, "I didn't know if you were home today, but I had some time, and I thought I'd come by and do some work on your landscaping before winter." Jan had no idea what I'd been thinking and feeling, but God knew. He was teaching me that I could trust him moment by moment, even for mundane needs.

■　■　■　■

In the days immediately after September 11, many well-meaning people tried to console me by saying, "Oh, this baby is going to be such a blessing. This child must have some special purpose; God must have some unique plan for this baby."

As much as I appreciated the kindness behind the statements, I rejected such thinking. *Yes, this child is special,* I'd think, *but no more so than David or Drew or any other baby born. They're all precious in God's sight, and he has a unique plan for every child.*

I'd had ultrasounds done, but Todd and I hadn't wanted to know the sex of the baby in advance, so I didn't change that decision. I still didn't know whether I was having a girl or a boy as I prepared to go to the hospital for the birth. I thought having a little girl would be wonderful, but then raising another boy might be easier. When things got tough, I could say, "Okay, you guys! Just go wrestle!"

The baby was due on January 15, but my doctor felt that inducing labor would give us more control, rather than risking my going into labor in the middle of the night. I agreed, and we decided to induce labor a week early.

I had never been big on having people with me in the birthing room. Todd alone had accompanied me for the birth of our boys. "You can come along as long as you stay quiet," I had teased him. He was pretty serious in the delivery room anyway and knew his job was just to be the strong, silent type for a few minutes while I concentrated on getting the real work done.

For the birth of this baby, I knew I'd need someone who could remind me of Todd and what his presence would have been. I decided to ask Melissa, Todd's sister, to be with me. Melissa loves babies and has had three children of her own, so I knew she could handle the birth experience. She's calm and strong, and her laid-back personality reminds me a lot of Todd's. Having her present in the delivery room would be the best stand-in for Todd on this earth.

■　■　■　■

Melissa flew in from Trenton, Michigan, the day before I was scheduled to give birth. My sister, Holly, had been staying with me during the last few days of my pregnancy, helping to watch the boys, so our plan was that Melissa would get me to the hospital and Holly would join us with Mom and the boys after the baby was born.

I woke up early on Wednesday, January 9, showered, and dressed in a comfortable maternity outfit. I put on my watch and my wedding ring, and then I slipped on the diamond tennis bracelet that Todd had bought for me in Florence, Italy, on September 8. What a priceless treasure that little bracelet had become to me!

We were supposed to be at the hospital by 7:00 A.M., so we planned on taking Holly's car and leaving the minivan for her so she could bring Mom and the boys later in the day. But when we attempted to start Holly's car, the engine just growled and wouldn't turn over. The battery was dead.

"Oh, this is not starting out well," I said to Melissa with a laugh. I woke up Holly and asked, "Is there any trick to starting your car?"

"Huh? No, why?"

Rather than take any chances, I gave her back her keys. Mom was coming later on, so I knew they'd have access to a car.

I slowly slid into the minivan and pointed Melissa in the direction of Princeton Medical Center. The hospital was expecting me, and everyone was extremely friendly when they saw me come in. We were escorted to a birthing room, where the labor nurse began asking me for logistical information. She entered my answers in the computer located beside the bed.

Checking in at the hospital brought all the post 9-11 emotions to a head for me. The nurse peppered me with all the usual questions a patient must answer when entering a hospital for nonemergency procedures. She wasn't doing anything wrong or invasive; she was simply doing her job. But as I answered her questions, once again the awful sense of aloneness overwhelmed me.

With our other children, Todd had been there for the admissions process, and *he* had answered all the questions. Now the simple procedure of filling out a medical questionnaire caused my emotions to erupt. Tears flowed freely down my face as I mourned Todd's absence.

Melissa stood quietly beside me. We held hands and cried together for a few minutes. The nurse waited patiently before continuing, and soon we were ready to begin the birthing process. Still, I worried privately, *How am I going to be able to have this baby under these circumstances?* I wondered if my body would even function properly and perform the way a birthing mother's body must.

We were soon to find out!

■ ■ ■ ■

The hospital staff broke my water and began administering Pitocin to induce labor. I stretched out on the hospital bed and tried to relax while we waited for the drug to take effect.

Chivon MacMillan visited after I had settled comfortably into the birthing room. She put her hands on my stomach, closed her eyes, and predicted jokingly, "The Amazing Kreskin says the baby will be 21 inches, weigh 6 pounds, 11 ounces, and it will be a girl."

Chivon's prediction was almost exactly on target! At 1:59 P.M., after an unimaginably easy labor (thanks in no small part to an epidural!), our baby was born: 7 pounds, 20 inches long, and, to Chivon's delight, a beautiful baby girl! I was so excited. I kept saying over and over, "I can't believe I had a girl!"

I named our daughter Morgan Kay Beamer. Her name is a combination of Todd's and my middle names. Of our three children, Morgan was the only one born with a full head of dark hair . . . just like Todd.

■ ■ ■ ■

My mom and Holly picked up David from school and
informed him that he now had a little sister, Morgan Kay.
During the drive to the hospital, David said to Mom and
Holly, "I really like the name Morgan. . . . I hope they don't
change her name."

David and Drew were so excited to see their new baby
sister. When they came into the hospital room and saw her
for the first time, they were wide-eyed. They kissed Morgan
so sweetly and gently, and I could already tell they were
going to be great big brothers.

They were both anxious to hold Morgan and passed her
back and forth as gently as little boys can—with Grandma
hovering close by all the time. At almost two years of age,
Drew's grasp of the English language was still minimal, but
he knew enough to say gleefully, "Baby! Baby!"

When it came time for David and Drew to go home, I
was holding Morgan against my chest. David came right to
the bed, leaned over, and spoke directly to Morgan, not to
me. "Morgan, we love you," he said. "We're gonna take
good care of you."

■ ■ ■ ■

When the news of Morgan's birth hit, again kind people
from around the world sent us all sorts of gifts. We were
deluged with cards and letters, teddy bears, more blankets,
even car seats and high chairs.

President Bush sent our baby a personal letter,

addressed to Morgan Kay herself, in which he was the first to tell her what she will no doubt hear throughout her life-time: "Your father was a hero on September 11, 2001. His selfless efforts to prevent additional loss of life on that tragic day reflected the best of the American spirit." Laura Bush sent Morgan a separate letter of welcome to the world.

More than 45 widows of the September 11 attack had given birth by the time Morgan was born. Many others who were pregnant at the time of the attack have given birth since then. I know their sorrow, but I also share their joy. Each of these new babies is a blessed reminder that God has chosen to give us another opportunity, another day to live, another chance to love.

29

THE BIGGER PICTURE

WE CELEBRATED DREW'S BIRTHDAY in February at Gymboree, and the guest of honor was his just-born sister, Morgan. With the birth behind me, I was more concerned than ever about rebuilding a happy, healthy life for our new family. That meant meeting the needs of my children, of course, but also ensuring I took care of myself, too. I knew I couldn't hope to raise my kids well if *I* was struggling to survive. My attitude was similar to the instructions flight attendants give to parents before a flight: if there's a problem, put on your own oxygen mask first, then help your children get adjusted.

Every Tuesday since November I'd been meeting with our church's professional counselor, Dr. Al Hickok—missing only one session for Morgan's birth. At our first meeting, I told him I'd considered myself a relatively healthy person before September 11 and wanted to make sure I continued to be one in the months and years ahead. I knew I needed an objective professional to assist me in sorting through all the thoughts, feelings, and responsibilities of my new circumstances.

Not surprisingly, I have high regard for counseling professionals. Since my mom is a professional counselor, and I've seen how she's helped so many people, I didn't have any qualms about seeking out a counselor myself. Dr. Al had encouraged Todd in his struggle to have a healthy attitude toward his work, and I hoped Dr. Al could provide insights on my struggles as well. I knew going through this process would be good not only for myself but also for my children—now and in the future.

One thing I've attempted to balance is the sadness I feel at losing Todd with the hope I have in knowing that this world is only the preparation for an eternity of joy beyond compare in heaven. Certainly I want my children to know God's promise of heaven, but I also want them to know it's okay to be sad that Todd's not with us right now. I let them see my tears but make sure we have lots of fun conversations about Todd, too. I don't want them to avoid talking about Todd for fear that every time his name is mentioned, "Mommy's going to start crying again!"

The pain is real, but so is the hope. Sometimes it's hard to live with both realities. For several weeks following September 11, I'd walk into Todd's closet, see his clothes, and start crying. Sometimes even now I go into the closet and close the doors. I crumple on the floor and, for a few minutes, just weep. I read the notes he wrote to me, touch his pillow, and wipe my tears with his T-shirt. I weep until there are no more tears, then take a deep breath, straighten myself up, and go back out to face whatever the day brings.

The tears still show up often in my life, sometimes when I least expect them. I know that even years from now, when the acute pain subsides, there will still be twinges of sadness because Todd's not here to enjoy life with us. But that's what life on this earth is—happiness mixed with sadness. True joy will never come here, but knowing it awaits me in eternity helps me progress through whatever life brings in the darkest of times. God has whispered two words to me over and over: *Look up. . . . Look up.* Through that quiet voice I'm reminded to look beyond my own little life to the Creator of the universe and what I know of his perspective. Without fail, looking up brings peace to my soul.

God has also provided constant reinforcement that Todd's story is making a difference in people's lives and that his death was not in vain. Nearly every week I get a letter from a stranger, telling me how Todd's words and the story of Flight 93 have affected that person. Individuals from all over the world have been changed for the good, forever, as a result of seeing Todd's faith in action.

One day, as I was talking to God, I said, "Lord, I know people have been impacted far and wide by Todd's life and his death. It would help, though, to know some people close by—people I can see every day—who have been affected. So when I'm having a bad day or the kids ask a hard question, I can see somebody whose life has been changed as a result of what has happened and know that it's been worth it." I guess in a strange way I wanted to know that Todd's sacrifice mattered not only in Washington, in other parts of the country, and around the world, but *around the block.*

And God met that need, too.

Some friends of ours were struggling to make a personal connection with God prior to September 11. One day, following Todd's death, the husband told me, "I've been on the fence in my relationship with God for a long time, not really going one way or the other. But I saw something in Todd that I wanted, and now I know I can't be on the fence anymore."

He has since accepted Jesus into his heart and life. Because of September 11 and Todd's response, both of these friends were propelled to think more deeply about trusting in God. And their lives have truly been changed. Todd's life was an encouragement and motivation to them, and now they are the same for me.

Also, during Todd's memorial service at our church I glanced around and noticed some old friends we hadn't seen in quite a while. I didn't get a chance to talk with them afterward, but on the way out, the wife told some mutual friends of Todd's and mine, "I don't know what Todd and Lisa have, but I don't have it, and I want that kind of relationship with God." The couple started attending our church, committed their lives to God, and now have a new perspective on what they're living for.

Perhaps the most personally rewarding result has been the impact Todd's life and death have had on some of the kids we used to teach in Sunday school class or in the youth group. Todd loved the kids so much and believed in them, and they loved him and trusted him. After Todd's death, Andrea Bredin, a girl in the youth group, wrote a special poem that expressed the sentiments of a lot of the kids:

I had a really cool friend, who became a martyr in the end.
A man of God was he, as anyone could plainly see.
He was very athletic and very tall,
With his gift, he played basketball.
A huge fan was he of the Chicago Bulls;
Pinball and posters of Michael kept his office full.
By faith he lived every single day;
When troubled he'd always first pray,
Then he would immediately take action,
Even if the direct result was not to his satisfaction.
He loved his wife and sons more than anything on earth;
Even though he's not here, he'll be looking over his third
    child's birth.
He always knew there was a greater plan,
And of that, God's will, he was a huge fan.
Todd was only of the young age of thirty-two,
When he last flew in that great sky of blue.
The nation's Capitol he forcefully saved,
Now America's flag and God's love are proudly waved.
He is in heaven, we know this to be true,
But Todd Beamer, we will always miss you.

Near the close of Todd's memorial service, Leonard Harris, one of the former youth-group members who is now in college, sang Ray Boltz's song "Thank You," a tribute to those who have impacted our lives in a positive way—Sunday school teachers, youth-group workers, missionaries, and others. Nowadays, undoubtedly, we would include police officers and firefighters in the list of true heroes. The essence of the song's lyrics is simple but poignant: "Thank you for giving to the Lord; I am a life that was changed."

During his rendition of the song, Leonard personalized the lyrics and sang them directly to Todd in heaven. In those lonely moments when I wonder why Todd was on the flight or why September 11 ever happened, I hear Leonard's heartwarming song. Then I smile and say to myself, *Thank you, Todd, for giving to the Lord . . . and thank you, Lord, for giving Todd to me.*

■　■　■　■

Lately I've been trying to look at the bigger picture, to discover what I'm supposed to learn from all this. I'm sure I have much growth yet to experience, but I've gleaned a few insights. Probably the most important truth is that my security must be in *God* rather than in anything or anyone in this world.

Think about it: the World Trade Center represented economic power, success, and security, yet it was shaken and destroyed in one hour or less. The Pentagon is the symbol of our nation's military might, yet it, too, proved vulnerable. Where can we find true security in these days?

The men and women in the Trade Center towers, the Pentagon, and aboard the four hijacked planes were some of the best our nation had to offer. They were the picture of intelligence, energy, and power. Yet their best wasn't good enough to keep the enemy from attacking, maiming, and killing several thousand people.

But I have found safety and security in a loving heavenly Father, who cannot be shaken, who will never leave me or forsake me, and in whom I can trust completely. For those looking for hope, I recommend grabbing the hand of your heavenly Father as tightly as possible, like a little child does with his parent. God is a hero who will *always* be there when you need him.

It's true that Todd and the other heroes aboard Flight 93 gave their lives that others might be saved. But if somehow they had known what was awaiting them, and they had been given a choice early that September morning, I doubt that any of them would have boarded that flight. Even in the midst of the hijacking, right down to the moment when Todd uttered his now-famous phrase, "Let's roll!" the true desire of his heart and that of Jeremy Glick, Tom Burnett, Mark Bingham, and all the others aboard Flight 93 was to somehow get home to their loved ones. They didn't want to die.

Yet there was one who came to earth, knowing ahead of time that his most important purpose in living would be accomplished only through his dying. He knew throughout his life and at the height of his career that no matter how well he performed, no matter how many people he helped, he was destined to die—to give his life so many others might find true life, abundant life here on earth, and eternal life in heaven to come.

But he really didn't want to die either. In fact, as he prayed in the garden of Gethsemane, just outside Jerusalem's city walls, Jesus begged God, "Father, if there is any other way . . . let this cup pass from me." He prayed so intensely that sweat ran like large drops of blood from his forehead. Think about that: even knowing all the good that was going to come as a result of his death, he prayed three times to avoid it: "If there is any other way . . ."

Finally he said, "Not my will but yours be done." That was God's plan.

I don't think Todd chose to die, but he did choose for God's will to be done in his life. Knowing that, he stepped into the aisle of that plane, trusting by faith that regardless of what happened, God would be true to his Word. Before he took that first step, Todd knew where he was going, even if he should die. He had built his life on a firm foundation.

Todd was not a Hollywood hunk or a comic-book superhero. He was an ordinary guy with ordinary faith in a great God. Not long ago I was going through some files on our computer and found Todd's description of his faith. He had been planning to do some short-term missions work with our church, and as part of the application, he had to write out his testimony. As I read it, I was once again impressed at his humility and how insignificant Todd thought he was in the eternal scheme of things. Todd wrote:

> I have had stops and starts in building my relationship with God. . . . I screw up, I let him down, and I do not always spend time with God the way I should. This is because I am trying to force the relationship and steer it in the direction I want it to go. That doesn't work, and only leads to frustration.
>
> However, each time I come to God to ask for forgiveness, he is there for me. Each time I ask God

for help and guidance, he is there for me. Each time
I cry out in frustration and pain, he is there for me.

While my relationship with God is far from
perfect . . . God has been there for me time and again,
and has expressed his love and grace for me.
Although at times I have taken God for granted . . .
my experience has been that God is patient and waiting for us to come to him. Once we come to him and
give more of our lives to him, he will give more of
himself to us.

What made Todd different from many other men who
are merely religious was not the fact that he was willing to
die for his faith; the terrorists did that! No, Todd was willing to *live* for his faith. Better still, he was willing to live
out his faith all the way to the end. Todd built his life on a
firm foundation so that when the storm came on September
11 he didn't have to check the blueprints to see if everything he had built his life on was going to stand. He
knew.

I was thinking about that in February, when I received a
call inviting me to speak at the 2002 National Prayer Breakfast in Washington. I wondered if I should accept the invitation. After all, the breakfast was attended by members of
Congress, international dignitaries, business and spiritual
leaders from all across our nation, and, of course, the president of the United States. What in the world did I have to
say to that group?

But once again, Mordecai's words to Esther echoed
across time: "For such a time as this . . ."

I accepted the invitation, and when I stood to speak to the group that day, I quoted the Scripture from Isaiah 40:30-31:

> *Even youths grow tired and weary,*
> *and young men stumble and fall;*
> *but those who hope in the Lord*
> *will renew their strength.*
> *They will soar on wings like eagles;*
> *they will run and not grow weary,*
> *they will walk and not be faint.*

I told them about seeing the hawk soaring above the crash site in Pennsylvania, and how God's peace had swept over me with the promise that for those who trust in him, he would renew their strength. "The peace that came even at that place in my life was because of my hope in the Lord," I told the august audience. "The difference between those who stumble and those who run is only the action of hoping in the Lord."

Then I told the prayer-breakfast group a story that Jesus had once told about two men who built new houses—one on the rock and one on the sand. When the storm came, the house on the sand fell with a great crash.[8] "The two houses were constructed of similar materials," I said, "and weathered similar storms, but the difference in the outcome was based on the foundation, the core."

If you live long enough, you're bound to encounter some rough storms. No one is immune to tragedy in this life. The house is the same, the storm is the same, but what

[8]See Matthew 7:24-27.

makes the difference is the foundation. Todd's foundation was securely built on his relationship with Jesus Christ. When everything in his life was shaken, his foundation remained sound. The question each of us must answer, sooner or later, is this: How secure is the foundation on which I'm building my life?

30

IT IS WELL
WITH MY SOUL

A FEW WEEKS after Todd's death, I was going through some papers in his office when I came across a quote by Theodore Roosevelt that Todd had kept at the bottom of his in-box for the past several years. Todd never discussed why the quote was meaningful to him, but looking at it that day in his office, it took on an entirely new significance.

> The credit belongs to the man who is actually in the arena . . . who strives valiantly, who knows the great enthusiasms, the great devotions, and spends himself in worthy causes. Who, at best, knows the triumph of high achievement and who, at worst, if he fails, fails while daring greatly so that his place shall never be with those cold and timid souls who know neither victory nor defeat.

On September 11 Todd Beamer completed his time on earth. His life ended while "daring greatly." He did not die with the "cold and timid souls who know neither victory nor defeat." He has even been called a hero for fighting back against evil, for putting his own life on the line in an attempt to save others.

While his final actions did require great courage, something else he did that morning required even more. In the face of the worst circumstances he could humanly imagine, Todd chose to rest in the words of the Lord's Prayer: "Thy will be done." He put himself in the hands of God, knowing that ultimately that was the only safe place to be. Of course Todd wanted to come home on September 11, but he knew if that didn't happen, God was still in control and would take care of him and of us.

Could God have prevented the atrocities of September 11 from being carried out? Absolutely! He is all-powerful and he hates evil. Could God have chosen to pull Todd off that plane? Absolutely! Miraculous stories abound of people who didn't make one of the hijacked flights or for some reason didn't get to the World Trade Center on that morning, as they had planned, and were spared. But I could drive myself crazy with all the "if onlys" and the "what if" questions. *If only Todd had taken another flight. . . . What if the plane had stayed on the ground in Newark another 10 minutes?* . . . Instead I must rest in the knowledge that, for some reason, God allowed these things to happen.

But even though God was in control, it was still human beings who were responsible for the murder of Todd and so many others on September 11. Am I angry and bitter toward them? It's a question people often ask.

Truthfully, if I were standing face-to-face with Osama

bin Laden or the men who hijacked the planes that day, my kickboxing practice might suddenly come into play. I'd have a hard time resisting some form of physical expression. Yet, at the same time, I've not had the time or the energy to waste harboring bitterness or resentment toward the perpetrators of the heinous attacks. I am concerned that, to the extent possible on earth, this evil is stopped and innocent people are protected. That's not my job, but I'm confident our nation and our allies will make sure this happens.

I know I can't change the tragedy of September 11 or even those who caused it. Ultimately, I can be responsible only for my own choices. The Bible says that God causes all things to work together for good—not that everything *is* good, but he will work it for good—to those who love God.[9] Todd didn't claim to be perfect, and neither do I, but we do fall into the category of those who love God. That means as we choose to trust God and follow his desire for our lives, he promises to work everything for good to us both now and in the future.

Although I never could have imagined the awful circumstances brought about in the life of my family by the events of September 11, I know that promise from God proved true for Todd on that day. God provided Todd with what he needed—strong teammates in his fellow passengers, a steady voice of reason in Lisa Jefferson, an opportunity to knowingly make a difference in the course of events, and, of course, after the crash of United Flight 93, the reality of heaven.

That promise proves true for me, too, as I go on from September 11. God has provided so many things: love

[9] See Romans 8:28.

beyond measure from family, friends, and strangers; the encouragement of knowing people whose lives have been changed because of Todd's example; glimpses of God's perspective on my life and on our world; and an unexplainable peace in my soul.

The words of an old hymn have come to mind so many times: *It is well, it is well with my soul.* I have known these words since I was a little girl, but not long ago I read the story about the man who wrote them. Horatio Spafford was a successful Chicago lawyer, a contemporary and friend of D. L. Moody, the famous preacher. In 1873 the family doctor recommended a vacation for Mrs. Spafford, so the couple planned a trip to Europe by ship.

Just before their departure, a matter came up that changed Mr. Spafford's plans. Rather than ruining the family vacation, Spafford sent his wife and four daughters on ahead, promising he would join them in a few days. Mrs. Spafford and the girls set sail for Europe without him.

On November 22, in a tragic, freak accident, the ship on which the women were traveling was rammed by an English vessel and sank in less than half an hour. With the cold, roaring waves of the Atlantic Ocean rolling over them, Mrs. Spafford and the girls were tossed from the ship as though they were tiny porcelain dolls. Mrs. Spafford was miraculously rescued, but all four girls drowned in the sea. Mrs. Spafford cabled her husband a stark message: "Saved alone."

Horatio Spafford bought passage aboard the first ship he could find that was sailing to England. Out on the high seas, the ship passed close to the spot where the accident had claimed the lives of his four daughters. With tears pouring down his face as he looked out over the rolling waves where his daughters had died, Horatio Spafford penned these words:

> When peace like a river attendeth my way,
> When sorrows like sea billows roll;
> Whatever my lot, Thou has taught me to say,
> "It is well, it is well with my soul."[10]

That was the song I requested be sung at Todd's memorial service on September 16. It was the song that went through my mind when I first stepped out of the bus at the crash site in Shanksville on September 17. I looked over at Todd's sister, Michele, and said, "He's not here." Nothing significant of Todd Beamer remained in that field in Pennsylvania. And he was more alive than ever at that very moment, enjoying a reality in heaven more incredible than anything we could hope to imagine on earth. He's in the presence of God himself! This heartfelt knowledge changed the devastation of that place into peace, and, as difficult as it may be for some to believe, even joy.

Michele nodded knowingly.

"Todd isn't here!" I said as much to myself as to anyone else who might be listening. I knew at that moment, *without a doubt*, that everything Todd and I believed and lived for was true.

My life since September 11 includes many human sorrows and challenges, and every day I must choose how

[10]"It Is Well with My Soul," copyright © 1873 by Horatio G. Spafford.

to confront them. I can sink into depression or anger or anxiety, or I can trust that God is working everything for my good. I have chosen to believe God—to believe he loves me and has a plan for now and for eternity. I don't claim to understand, but I choose daily—even moment by moment—to have faith not in what is seen but in what is unseen. The road ahead is uncertain and even scary at times, but I believe that God will provide what's best for me, just when I need it. Even now, in the midst of great sorrow, there is much to be thankful for—a great family, wonderful friends, and a strong community of faith. I try to appreciate my blessings every day.

Of course the three sweetest gifts are often gathered on my lap. To them, "Let's roll!" is not a slogan, a book, or a song; it's a lifestyle. A lifestyle Todd and I began together . . . and one my children and I will carry on. Each time I hear those words, Todd's voice calls out once again to the children and me, letting us know it's time to set out on another adventure. Our journey is different now, but it's still one of hope, faith, and a knowledge of our ultimate destination.

One day shortly before Christmas, just a few months after Todd's death, I was halfheartedly unpacking some holiday decorations. Evidently I wasn't moving fast enough for David, who was excited to put the stockings up on the fireplace. So he looked at me and, in a playful voice reminiscent of his father, said, "Come on, Mom! Let's roll!"

I fought back the tears for a moment, and then said with a little grin, "You're right, David. Let's roll!"

It is well . . . it is well . . . with my soul.

Are you ready? Okay. Let's roll.

ALL THE HEROES OF UNITED FLIGHT 93

CREW

Lorraine G. Bay
flight attendant

Sandra W. Bradshaw
flight attendant

Jason Dahl
captain

Leroy Homer
first officer

CeeCee Ross-Lyles
flight attendant

PASSENGERS

CHRISTIAN ADAMS

TODD BEAMER

ALAN BEAVEN

MARK BINGHAM

DEORA BODLEY

MARION BRITTON

THOMAS BURNETT, JR.

WILLIAM CASHMAN

GEORGINE CORRIGAN

PATRICIA CUSHING

JOSEPH DELUCA

PATRICK DRISCOLL

EDWARD FELT

JANE FOLGER

COLLEEN FRASER

ANDREW "SONNY" GARCIA

JEREMY GLICK

LAUREN GRANDCOLAS

WANDA A. GREEN

DONALD F. GREENE

LINDA GRONLUND

RICHARD GUADAGNO

TOSHIYA KUGE

HILDA MARCIN

WALESKA MARTINEZ

NICOLE MILLER

LOUIS J. NACKE

DONALD A. PETERSON

JEAN HOADLEY PETERSON

MARK ROTHENBERG

CHRISTINE SNYDER

JOHN TALIGNANI

HONOR ELIZABETH WAINIO

DEBORAH A. WELSH

KRISTIN GOULD WHITE

THE
TODD M. BEAMER
FOUNDATION . . .

*Seeks to
equip children
experiencing
family trauma
to make
heroic choices
every day.*

**The
Todd M. Beamer
Foundation**

CHILDREN TODAY face an uncertain world. However, no matter what our future holds, they—and we—will always need heroes. That's why, in honor of Todd's life and the legacy he left behind, I, his wife, along with family and friends, founded the Todd M. Beamer Foundation. Inspired by Todd's passion for developing character, faith, and courage in the lives of young people, the Foundation focuses especially on those children who lost a parent on September 11.

IT'S OUR GOAL at the Foundation to help today's children grow into a new generation of everyday heroes—people willing to sacrifice themselves for the good of others. By investing in programs designed to support parents and nurture children, we look forward to seeing our goal realized . . . and lives changed.

LISA BEAMER
FOUNDER

DOUGLAS A. MacMILLAN
EXECUTIVE DIRECTOR

To learn how you can help continue Todd's legacy and develop heroes for tomorrow, please contact:

THE TODD M. BEAMER MEMORIAL
FOUNDATION, INC.
P.O. Box 32
Cranbury, NJ 08512
(866) BEAMER23
www.beamerfoundation.org

ABOUT THE AUTHORS

LISA BEAMER, a homemaker, mother, and the widow of Todd Beamer, has become an enduring symbol of grace and courage in troubled times. She has generated major media interest, including appearances on *Larry King Live, 60 Minutes,* and *Oprah,* as well as feature stories in *Time, Newsweek,* and the *New York Post.* Recently she was selected by *People* magazine as one of the "25 Most Intriguing People of 2001" for the way she has spoken "eloquently of the need to move on in life without hatred." She lives in the United States with her two young sons and infant daughter.

KEN ABRAHAM is a professional writer with world-class credentials. Recent projects include *Payne Stewart,* the *New York Times* best-seller he co-authored with golfer Payne Stewart's widow, Tracey, and *Zinger!,* the autobiography of Paul Azinger.